Service in the AI Era

Service in the AI Era

Science, Logic, and Architecture Perspectives

Jim Spohrer, Paul P. Maglio,
Stephen L. Vargo, and Markus Warg

BEP
BUSINESS EXPERT PRESS
Leader in applied, concise business books

Service in the AI Era: Science, Logic, and Architecture Perspectives

Copyright © Business Expert Press, LLC, 2023.

Cover design by Charlene Kronstedt

Interior design by Exeter Premedia Services Private Ltd., Chennai, India

First published in 2022 by
Business Expert Press, LLC
222 East 46th Street, New York, NY 10017
www.businessexpertpress.com

ISBN-13: 978-1-63742-303-5 (paperback)
ISBN-13: 978-1-63742-304-2 (e-book)

Business Expert Press Service Systems and Innovations for Business and Society Collection

First edition: 2022

10 9 8 7 6 5 4 3 2 1

Description

Are you prepared for the coming AI era? AI advances will profoundly change your daily service interactions, so this book provides readers with *a necessary understanding of service, the application of resources (e.g., knowledge) for the benefit of another.* In just minutes, you can learn about today's use of early-stage AI for automation and augmentation, and essential elements of **service science, service-dominant (S-D) logic, and Service Dominant Architecture (SDA).**

Ultimately, improved service *for all* is possible with human-level AI and digital twins—but requires investing wisely in better models: Better models of the world both complex natural and social systems (science), better mental models in people to improve interactions (logic), better cultural and structural models of organizations to improve change (architecture), and better trusted and responsible AI models. *The service innovation community studies and builds better models to improve interactions and change in business and society.*

The book challenges all responsible actors—individuals, businesses, universities, and governments—**to invest systematically and wisely to upskill with AI (the X+AI vision).** The service innovation community is a growing transdiscipline harnessing all disciplines to become better T-shaped professionals. Extensive end notes, bibliography, and index are provided.

Keywords

artificial intelligence; AI; service innovation; service science; service-dominant (S-D) logic; Service Dominant Architecture (SDA); digital twins; upskilling; T-shaped professionals

Contents

Acknowledgments...ix

Prologue..xi

Introduction...xvii

Part I   Service in the AI Era 1
Chapter 1   Foundations of AI: Automation and Augmentation........3
Chapter 2   Service Robots and Platform Society...........................5
Chapter 3   Questions 9

Part II   Science.. 11
Chapter 4   Foundations of the Sciences....................................13
Chapter 5   Service Science 15
Chapter 6   Questions 21

Part III   Logic... 25
Chapter 7   Foundations of Logics and Dominant Logics.............27
Chapter 8   Service-Dominant Logic..29
Chapter 9   Questions 33

Part IV   Architecture 35
Chapter 10   Foundations of Architectures and Dominant
             Architectures 37
Chapter 11   Service Dominant Architecture..................................39
Chapter 12   Questions 43

Service in the AI Era Revisited...45

Conclusion 55

End Notes 59

References...105

About the Authors..123

Index 125

Acknowledgments

To our *big tent* service community and the International Society of Service Innovation Professionals (ISSIP.org); to scholars, educators, reflective practitioners, and all students of service, who like us find service a wonderful phenomenon that is worthy of deeper study. Special thanks to Terri Griffith, Clara Bassano, Shaun West, and other anonymous reviewers for detailed comments that helped further simplify, clarify, and connect parts of this work.

Prologue

All roads lead to *service*. As you will see, it connects you with the world, and it is the glue that connects important concepts in business and society. Arguably, service is quickly becoming the central concept of our time, as service offerings become infused with advanced technologies like *artificial intelligence (AI)* and scale to new levels of quality, productivity, compliance, and sustainable innovation.

The Centrality of Service

Why is service so central to human history—so connected to every other important concept? In this short book, you will see that *service is the application of resources* (e.g., knowledge) *for the benefit of another*. Service is the *basis of exchange* (e.g., social, economic). Service is at *the core of value cocreation*—which makes every situation more beneficial and win-win for everyone involved. Service underlies social and economic development, and the wealth of people, businesses, and nations. Simply put, service connects each of us to the world around us.

In terms of connectedness, the term *service* is like the actor Kevin Bacon; seemingly everything in our human world throughout history connects to *service* in just a few steps. In popular culture, the Kevin Bacon Game is played by movie buffs who compete to show off their knowledge of how all other actors and movies connect to Kevin Bacon in just a few steps (usually less than six to eight connections). We will show that human actors applying knowledge to help others is a central concept and connects to:

- Value—what humans value, and *the capability to make and keep promises* or in more technical jargon, *value propositions*, when people interact and cocreate value.
- People—*physical human actors* in biological bodies filling societal roles that possess rights to access resources used in value propositions; helping and being helped by others.

- Organizations—*virtual human actors* with specific purposes, such as businesses, governments, universities, and all types of *enterprises*, with in-network/ecosystem roles and possessing access rights to resources used in value propositions.
- Institutions (e.g., norms, symbols, conventions, rules)—institutional arrangements (i.e., sets of interrelated institutions) are *coordination mechanisms* that guide actor actions and interactions.
- Technology—human actors as tool makers, creating new resources.
- Information—human actors as symbol makers, manipulators and communicators, keeping track of resources and promises kept and broken.
- Cooperation—human cultural evolution and prosocial capabilities to solve larger scale challenges, with networks of people, technology, organizations, and information.
- Learning—development of human actors' capabilities to share and improve knowledge, resources, and prosocial norms; sometimes called *upskilling* in times of rapid change.
- Knowledge—human actors use the scientific method to create *better models of the world*, new resources and competencies by more deeply understanding *phenomena* in the world.
- Resources—how humans see and make use of the capabilities the world has to offer.
- Trust—human ability to interact responsibly with strangers in complex ways while keeping promises, and to create value propositions with *win-win outcomes* (or in technical jargon, *nonzero-sum games*).
- Identity—how humans see themselves, based on memories and aspirations.
- Reputation—how humans see others, based on experiences and expectations.
- Models—how humans simplify *complex systems with many interacting parts that change over time*, including improving *AI models of the world*.

- Civilization—human history, and the growing awareness of better designed win-win (or nonzero sum) interactions, responsibly making and keeping promises.

How does service connect you to your world today? How will those connections change in the AI era? As AI accelerates scientific discoveries, new resources and new types of service are becoming possible for the first time.

The Phenomenon of Service

You depend on the existence of service as a phenomenon in the world many times every day to live comfortable and productive lives. Saying "you depend on service" is like saying you depend on human interaction and trusting that other people will continue to act responsibly and keep their promises. Certainly, technology failing everywhere would be bad, but service failing everywhere would be a disaster. More practically speaking, consider that from the moment you wake up and turn on the lights and use running water (utilities), travel or use smartphones (transportation and communication), make purchases (retail, finance), see a doctor (health care), learn through an online course (education), watch a movie or listen to a song (entertainment), eat at a restaurant or stay in a hotel (hospitality), or renew a driver's license (government)—you depend on diverse service offerings and contribute consciously or unconsciously to the realization of their associated value propositions. All of which can be viewed as the application of resources (e.g., knowledge) that is mutually beneficial to the customer and the provider. But what about all the other *stakeholders*, not just the customer and provider? People ask this question, because of the interconnectedness of all this service to the environment, to skills, and to jobs. The world of service is becoming increasingly dependent on responsible and trusted stewards to ensure technology plays its role as promised, without unintended consequences.

Service (like life itself) is both fundamental and diverse, which makes it hard to get everyone to agree on a single definition. *Life requires resources—* such as matter, energy, space, and time—but only certain dynamic configurations (*living biological system entities*) exhibit the phenomenon of life. *Service requires resources*—such as people, technology, information, organizations—but only certain dynamic configurations (*interacting and changing service system responsible actors*) exhibit the phenomenon of service, applying knowledge to consciously make and keep mutually beneficial promises, guided in part by institutional arrangements. In business and society, the payoff of *service innovation is improved interaction and change processes*—or more simply, new ways of helping others that improve quality of life. The purpose of service innovation is to find new ways that people can apply knowledge for mutual beneficial interactions that improve the quality of life and well-being. The challenge is to also ensure freedom, justice, inclusion, diversity, privacy, and alignment with human values and happiness (which are culturally dependent and evolving) as well as to ensure sustainability and resilience (which are somewhat more objective but also evolving). Like the *agile work practice* that emphasizes *improving improvement processes*, and which is popular in business and government today, most actors are trying to start from where they are and transform into better future versions of themselves (identities and reputations). Like the *positive mindset* for learning and change that is also popular in business and government today, the competition to improve is largely a competition with *oneself* to become that better future self.

Expectations about service change over time. With every passing generation and each new technological era or crisis (e.g., pandemic, war, natural disaster), older types of service are transformed, new types of service appear, and often higher expectations about quality, sustainability, personal safety, and other characteristics of service become the new normal.

No matter how you define it, service exists—and it exists in growing abundance in the human world, fueled in part by AI advances. *Service is worthy of study by scholars (science), worthy of teaching by educators (logic), and worthy of mastery by practitioners who put their unique forms of expertise into practice through business and government structures (architecture).* Implicit in all definitions are *responsible actors, interactions, and outcomes*—an *evolving ecology* in fact—but we are getting ahead of ourselves.

The Coming AI Era

This book explores service in the AI era. *AI* is a hot topic these days. Driverless cars, robot surgeons, image recognition, speech recognition, language translation, and more sophisticated prototypes and more *deployed machine capabilities* are appearing every month. Advances in applying deep learning and increasing availability of large datasets, as well as massive computational resources, make it possible for machines to finally *learn* to perform a range of perception tasks *at or above human-level capabilities.*

While getting AI to near human-like levels across the board is still decades away, eventually AI may enable virtual humans (of a sort) who can be *trusted socially* and *take responsibility for their actions and interactions.* Some believe this is about two generations away (about 40 years, or 2060), while others see it as at least ten generations away or believe it will never happen.

Even if you doubt virtual humans (of any sort) will ever happen, increasing AI capabilities are poised to have a big impact on the application of knowledge for mutual benefits; this fact has great relevance to all three perspectives on service explored in this book. The opportunities and challenges of service in the AI era can be best explored given a basic understanding of AI and *science, logic, and architecture perspectives on service*—hence this book.

Three Perspectives

This concise book is for a general audience, busy people who are curious about the world, who are outside the service research community. We know there is a lot of interest in the topic of *service in the AI era* from students and professionals working in science, education, business, and government. AI advances depend on machines with *better models of the world.* The *three perspectives* presented in this book also deal with models. First, *models of the world (science);* second, *models in people's minds (logic); and* third, *models embedded in organizations' structures and cultures (architecture).* We are primarily writing for scholars (who help expand useful knowledge), educators (who help the next generation learn), practitioners (who use their expertise to get work done, often as part of organizations). In the body of this book, we keep it concise, and for those who want to go deeper, we provide endnotes and bibliography. We hope each perspective—science, logic, architecture—has something for everyone, especially science for those interested in becoming researchers, logic for everyone who wants to think differently about service and get better at sharing a powerful way of looking at the world, and architecture for those who want to start a new venture (entrepreneurs) or transform and restructure an existing business department or government agency (enterprise architects, public policymakers).

Colleagues, Community, and Context

Chances are you are a service professional, working in health care, education, government, retail, hospitality, law enforcement, the military, consulting, caregiving, managing, leading, or some role where you are required to apply knowledge and know-how in a responsible way to help others and keep learning (*upskilling*). At the dawn of this new era in AI, it is a good time for service professionals and the service research community to take stock, broaden access to what is already known, and importantly, re-examine and re-frame what is left to do. There is no shortage of questions and no shortage of opportunities, especially in the *big tent* of disciplines and perspectives of the service community (short for communities of practice). *A community of practice can be defined as a group of people who share common interests or concerns and develop methods of working and learning together to achieve common goals.* In discussions with colleagues at conferences, interest in AI has skyrocketed in recent years. And though service practice and research conferences, journals, and professional associations come in dozens of shapes and sizes, there is always more to do to make the big tent even bigger and more representative of disciplines and cultures needed to navigate service in the AI era.

Words are tools. Education and philosophical foundations are key to building strong communities of practice, dominated by understanding, trust, and value cocreation—service. The International Society of Service Innovation Professional (ISSIP) created two concise book collections with Business Expert Press (BEP) to deepen the readers' understanding of service systems as well as collective intelligence. In this short book, we aim to provide a concise summary of progress so far, along the way strengthening some of the foundations and looking toward future opportunities and challenges. We hope you enjoy it. We hope you find it both accessible for the short term (an easy read that provides a good map of the territory) and handy for the long term (with extensive notes and bibliography if you want to go deeper).

Introduction

This concise book is written for busy people who are curious about the world around them.

Interactions and Change

Daily life is full of interactions. For busy people, every hour of the waking day is full of all types of interactions. For busy people who are curious about the world, every interaction is a learning experience. Some interactions have good outcomes for everyone involved, while other interactions have outcomes that are not so good for some stakeholders. We, the authors of this book, are members of a growing community that is trying to learn all we can about these daily interactions of busy people. *Put simply, our goal includes understanding better both the good and bad days.* A better understanding can help people, businesses, and even nations improve interactions, resulting in more good outcomes for everyone's well-being and quality of life. That good feeling of win-win outcomes from our daily interactions is worth a lot to everyone. Not surprisingly, we have learned that *great* interactions create more value for everyone, all the stakeholders gain. Everyone comes away from the interaction a winner in some way. Terrible interactions generate waste in some form, sometimes even the tragedy of wasted human potential. As specialists who often use seemingly complex jargon, our goal in this book is to distill and share the most general and important ideas concisely and with the broadest possible audience of busy, curious people.

What is one of the biggest challenges in trying to improve interactions for everyone? Change. Improving anything requires changing from old ways of thinking and doing to new ways of thinking and doing. Changing habits is often stressful. *Changing habits of mind, the way you think about the world can be especially challenging.* Also, history is full of examples of change that helped some people, while making life much worse for others at the same time. Individuals and groups experience change differently.

For example, younger people and older people may see change very differently. People from different cultures or family backgrounds may see change very differently. People who have spent years making a living for themselves and their families doing a particular type of work in a particular way will surely see change differently if the change negatively impacts their ways of working and providing for their family. Poorly planned change can also have unintended consequences. This is especially true in a world where seemingly everything is connected.

The specialists who spend their days trying to solve this puzzle of understanding and improving daily interactions have a name. They are known as the *service research community*. Thousands of people from around the world do this work, and they have jobs in big companies and small companies, in large and small government agencies, and in universities and nonprofits as well. We could share with you their stories, and the unlikely paths that lead them—including each of us—from other careers to join the *big tent* service research community. After reading this book, we hope some of you may want to join the community as well and adopt some new ways of thinking about interactions and change in your daily lives. *All people have experiences to share about good interactions and good change, as well as bad interactions and bad change.*

What unites our diverse and global service research community is a commitment to better understanding daily interactions and helping people, businesses, and governments change in a way that as much as possible: (1) increases the number of good days, in which busy people experience that win-win well-being feeling from interactions; (2) ensuring the changes help everyone; and (3) all the while avoiding unintended consequences. While many of you may think *STOP* now, and conclude this is an *IMPOSSIBLE* task, remember that there are millions of specialists working on smaller improvements in their corners of the world. Billions of dollars are being invested in smaller improvements. We will return to this concern of the *impossibility* of the task later in this book, but some groundwork must be put in place first.

In the remainder of this introduction, we briefly introduce service and AI with a bit more jargon, which will be explained more fully in later chapters. The intention is to simply give a sense of how service and AI, two jargony terms, are becoming increasingly intertwined. They are becoming intertwined for the simple reason that a lot of the improvement investments being made by businesses and governments are in new technology innovations to improve service. Every day, more busy people are using smartphones apps and online platforms to get things done. Online platforms have been defined as a digital service or technology-enabled service that enables "interactions between two or more distinct but interdependent sets of users (whether firms or individuals) who interact through the service via the Internet." In jargon, this is called technology-mediated service interactions—and with robots on the horizon, technology-mediated service interactions are about to go into *monster truck* overdrive.

Businesses and governments are investing heavily to insert more AI into both essential and mundane service offerings, changing the way people interact to get things done in daily life. Change and what not to change is a concern of individuals as well as leaders of businesses and nations. Change brings opportunity, but also brings fears of hazards that need to be better understood. Data-driven, science-based service innovations that drive out cost and sometimes concentrate control continue to shape the new architecture of business and government that provisions service to customers and citizens. *We challenge you to try to think of any service (daily interaction) that is not the subject of improvement investment (change).* Even grabbing a morning coffee and breakfast biscuit at the local drive through is being analyzed for change—all types of routine daily interactions are being studied. Still, there are many questions to be asked by the service research community, and multiple possible answers to be explored. So, let's begin. This book offers a concise entry point into service in the AI era from three perspectives: science, logic, and architecture. In just a few pages, let's come to a basic understanding of how simple these really are in essence. Let's replace any lingering jargon fear with a basic understanding.

AI Comes to Service

AI is always in the news. It is hard to miss. *By AI, we mean technologies that can act intelligently (like people in some ways) in real-world contexts, whether by learning from data or by being programmed by people or both.* The service research community has always been intensely interested in technological change. And many have already begun exploring the implications of AI for service from their own perspectives, for example, service robots in retail and hospitality, or the shift in the workforce toward jobs in *the feeling economy*. Yet, questions about AI abound. Mixed in with the basic questions you have come to expect about service (e.g., where is the science? why it is dominant? architecture for what?), on the rise is a steady stream of questions about advancing AI capabilities and the implications for service professionals and the service research community.

Views on AI remain mixed. Some see doom and gloom. Others imagine near utopia with people freed from traditional labor all together. All in all, this diversity of opinion is exactly what you would expect from the *big tent* service community. Communities work together to build ideas. These ideas shape and are shaped by professional practice—the craft of practitioners, scholars, and educators in the professional communities. Terms are borrowed, terms are used, terms are thrown away, new terms are invented, and occasionally, some new terms stick.

Service Comes to AI

Trust, responsibility, cocreation, and *ethics* are four key terms that are all core to the *big tent* service community but relatively new in the AI community, from an investment and competitive differentiator perspective. As AI enters the adoption stage in business and society, customers and citizens are demanding trusted AI that works well in tandem with people and is demonstrably fair, unbiased, secure, and explainable. Those who develop and deploy AI systems must take responsibility for quality and regulatory compliance of real-world service offerings, not simply the expected productivity gains of innovative laboratory prototypes. Also, when it comes to cocreation with people and machines, ways of interaction are being changed; intelligent augmentation of people and organizations using AI systems is reshaping interactions to mean something new.

The *democratization of AI* means that every economic actor will be paired with an AI capability booster. *The shift to X+AI pairs is to improve X's interaction capabilities.* Therefore, AI is being infused into more and more interactions. For example, during the pandemic, many people used Zoom's AI transcription feature, or automatic meeting notes, to save time taking notes as well as have an easily searchable record of the conversation. So, start thinking about customer + AI, not just provider + AI. Any AI tool an employer provides an employee to improve productivity may eventually find its way to the customer to use in self-service mode. In fact, platform owners (employer + AI) who are competing with other platforms for both employees and customers may work to align better employee + AI and customer + AI investments as a growth strategy. As *upskilling* people is required for high-skill, high-pay jobs, learners + AI and educators + AI will also be increasingly common, including earning while learning on smartphone apps connected to online platforms, so (l)earner + AI and platform + AI.

Beyond using terms such as trust, responsibility, cocreation, and ethics, another connection point between the service and AI communities is policy implications for skills, jobs, and inclusiveness. Will people + AI *earn and invest more* and become increasingly wealthy? AI-empowered earners in a platform society with responsible platforms helping people earn more and more, as the platform owners are competing for collaborators by expanding both upskilling and earning opportunities—*sometimes abbreviated as (l)earning—both learning and earning.* (L)earning opportunities on responsible platforms help grow the eminence of participants. Others fear AI-empowered businesses and nations exploit people. *Earning and spending that does not increase retirement investing is increasingly seen as an exploitive, poverty trap.* Some predict AI infusion will accelerate winner-take-all dynamics—or at least winner-take-most dynamics, growing the division in society between the haves and the have-nots. Reshaping interactions to provide both for today and tomorrow for all stakeholders is a challenge.

Growing Connections That Strengthen Both

All of the connections described briefly between the service and AI communities of practice are the result of what people *value most*, not simply the result of technological progress. Human-centered design and human values are becoming a topic of growing importance to scholars, educators, and practitioners (in industry and in government) alike, especially given so many cultural and ideological variations. In recent days, too often, we hear people say, "I just don't understand people like 'them' and how they think about the world—do you?"

What do we mean by *human values* and *human-centered design*? While not always explicit, the notion of human values and human-centered design pervades all the sections that follow on science, logic, and architecture perspectives. Human values deal with issues of the individual and the collective, wealth and poverty, freedom and security, justice and fairness, inclusion and exploitation, and opportunities to develop greater capabilities and take on more ambitious goals, often called *upskilling*, not just well-being, but well-becoming opportunities. A human-centered design not only improves the experience of the individual human actors directly involved in *interaction and change processes,* but aims to consider implications for all stakeholders as well as potential, longer-term unintended consequences. *Processes are simply ways of getting things done, and a human-centered design aims to improve the ways things get done aligned with human values.*

Is AI like a *bicycle for the mind*, both taking you further than walking and strengthening your muscles in case you need to walk? Or is AI like a *car for the mind*, taking us much further faster, but in the long run, weakening our ability to walk? Also consider that bicycles are more affordable to more people than cars. Bicycles can go more places and require less investment in infrastructure. The point being that depending on human values—those ideas embraced by responsible nations, businesses, and individuals—the future directions of service and AI progress can look profoundly different. In the coming AI era, as AI becomes more capable, and infused in more service offerings, does the use of AI make people stronger or weaker?

In the end, human values come down to questions. What are the individual and collective aspirations that guide people toward a shared future? How do people work together to raise and answer some tough and possibly uncomfortable questions? For example, questions about taking responsibility for building not just a smarter (more efficient and effortless, thoughtless change) world but a wiser (more inclusive and meaningful, thoughtful change) world? How can fear be replaced with understanding? Mere survival, day-to-day living replaced with more meaningful, multi-generational, and sustainable living?

PART I

Service in the AI Era

Civilization advances by extending the number of important operations which we can perform without thinking of them.
—Alfred North Whitehead, *English Mathematician*

We tend to overestimate the effect of a technology in the short run and underestimate the effect in the long run.
—Roy Amara, *Amara's Law*

Machines will be capable, within twenty years, of doing any work that a man can do.
—Herbert A. Simon, 1965, in *The Shape of Automation for Men and Management*

There was a need to give this field a formal name because work on intelligent machines was done by many individuals and organizations but under different names, that produced friction in knowledge transfer and collaborations.
—Zizu, 2018, a fictional AI, asking humans about its origins and receiving their responses

I am putting myself to the fullest possible use, which is all I think that any conscious entity can ever hope to do.
—HAL 9000 from *2001: A Space Odyssey.*

For thousands of years, we have known the perils of getting exactly what we wished for. In every story where someone is granted three wishes, the third wish is always to undo the first two wishes.
—Stuart Russell, 2019, in *Human Compatible: Artificial Intelligence and the Problem of Control*

We've been waiting decades—maybe even centuries—for the ability to reverse Baumol's Cost Disease in our most service-heavy, yet most critical, industries, such as healthcare... But Baumol himself couldn't have foreseen the revolution that AI is creating...

—Vijay Pande, *general partner at Andreessen Horowitz.*

CHAPTER 1

Foundations of AI

Automation and Augmentation

While its roots go back further, as a field of study and community of practice, artificial intelligence (AI) was formally named and began at a Dartmouth, New Hampshire workshop in 1956. From the outset, two camps emerged—those whose primary focus was technology-centric automation (making more capable generations of *thinking* machines) and those focused on human-centric augmentation (making more capable generations of *thinking* people in partnership with machines). The automation camp imagined someday having a machine that imitated a person so well that judges could not tell the difference between machine and human. Meanwhile, the augmentation camp imagined super-professionals solving complex and urgent problems beyond the reach of the best minds of the day. Both camps had utopian advocates and dystopian critics, while the reality was slow and steady progress, punctuated with so-called *AI winters* of waning interest and investment, and *AI summers* of increased enthusiasm and investment. Progress in deep learning is the cause of the current AI summer. Deep learning requires huge datasets and massive amounts of computing power to solve a math problem and build better AI.

As both agriculture and manufacturing were mechanized and scaled in the 1800s and 1900s, the automation AI camp envisioned scaling access to complex, knowledge-intensive service, increasing access to the capabilities provided by doctors, teachers, musicians, actors, lawyers, and someday perhaps even those in political offices. Meanwhile, the augmentation AI camp envisioned empowering human professionals, allowing them to solve previously unsolvable complex and urgent problems for science, business, and society. AI can be used to improve productivity by replacing labor with technology to get routine service work done more quickly and cheaply, and AI can be used to improve quality and creativity by augmenting the performance of people who care about quality and innovation.

In short, like two sides of the same coin, both automation and augmentation can lead to better AI and better service. This better service viewpoint may provide a more integrated view of these two AI camps. Both camps offer better scaling of service. In later sections, we also explore what the service community of practice has to offer the AI community of practice. In the next section, we explore the reality of service robots (automation) and service platforms (augmentation). Service robots go beyond self-service technologies (SSTs) into the realm of super-service. Service platforms empower superior performance and super-professionals. As we argue, platforms can empower customer self-service or can be used by employees or partners to augment their professional service-providing capabilities.

CHAPTER 2

Service Robots and Platform Society

In the previous chapter, we learned that better AI, both automation and augmentation, cuts the cost of scaling up better service. *Scaling up means easier access to innovation; put simply, it means more people, in more places, have more affordable access to a service offering.* This section looks at two examples of service in the AI era. Thousands of other examples or *AI use cases* exist and more are constantly being created by workers today in both business and government. These workers are in jobs that require high-skill and offer high pay. More and more offering managers (practitioners) do this kind of work to create AI use cases, as AI capabilities improve from investments, and new uses need to be found to accelerate return on investment (ROI). The use cases can also be thought of as improved service offerings and therefore as data-driven, science-based, technology-enabled service innovations that need to be properly orchestrated into existing systems architectures and properly marketed and managed to accelerate ROI. *Service is a lens for busy, curious people to see the world more clearly as it is unfolding today.*

Service Robots

Most service robots in the home do not have arms or legs yet, just *ears* (microphones), *mouths* (speakers), and an Internet connection. From Siri to Alexa, they can act on simple commands ("What will the weather be like today?"). Roomba can roll around cleaning floors. More sophisticated service robots are on the way to help in homes and in businesses. For example, large retail warehouse chains have streams of customers entering stores on a find-and-buy mission. Numerous alternative best practices exist to help customers on their journey, including greeters at the entrance and QR codes to download mobile apps and access information on demand. Service robots are increasingly available with speech recognition ("I need to find"), vision recognition ("I need to replace this"), or touchscreens embedded to help customers. In addition to retail stores, service robots are appearing in airports, hotel lobbies, hospitals, sporting events, and a wide range of venues that offer information desks staffed with docents (knowledgeable staff). Regarding adoption of AI in customer service contexts, these systems face both technical barriers (performance over a wide range of customer requests) as well as social barriers (concerns by employees of job loss).

Using tele-robotics, a person can monitor and control a service robot, which addresses some of the technical and social barriers to the adoption of service robots. Tele-robotics is simply remote control of a robot, from toy cars to flying drones to robot miners to transatlantic surgery, tele-robotics scales up access to innovations. Because a skilled person can operate a small fleet of tele-robots simultaneously, tele-robot operator is a next generation, high-tech job. A skilled operator can remotely interact with customers to handle situations that a service robot cannot handle on its own, which also creates training data to improve service robots over time. *Training data* is what today's AI systems need to *learn* to do things better—the more data, the better the performance on a narrow task. Tele-robots can also come in the form of drones for use outdoors in open spaces, such as national parks where hikers may be lost or encountering difficulties. Tele-robots augment human performance, while generating data to improve robotics (automation). Therefore, tele-robots illustrate that augmentation and automation are two sides of the same coin across a wide range of customer contact situations.

To further illustrate the way in which augmentation and automation are two sides of the same coin, consider one of the fastest growing segments of service robots, home robots. Robots in the home may be a cost-effective way to reduce human labor in the home. Homes come with many chores (time cost), which can be outsourced to cleaners, cooks, home repairs, lawn maintenance, pantry restocking, and other service providers (money cost). By some estimates, over 10 percent of family income is spent on in-home services that may be eventually provided by service robots at a fraction of the cost.

As technical and social barriers are overcome, service robots will be available to automate or augment workers—and to reduce the need for jobs when they lower the cost of living for homeowners. Lowering the cost of living for homeowners is especially important for elderly people approaching retirement age. Home health care robotics is an active area of research in many developed nations with large elderly populations.

Platform Society

Most younger people cannot imagine life without their smartphones. Smartphone apps connected to online platforms are a type of digital service that is increasingly used to support interactions. *Digital service* uses computer technology for easy access and collects user data to automatically improve service over time—often with the help of AI. Some of the largest investors in AI use cases are traditional and platform businesses that have successfully increased *customer engagement* with mobile apps. The business models of social media and online gaming platforms may depend on active, loyal customers with daily interaction patterns that are as high as possible—this is *customer engagement.* Unhealthy levels, or even addiction behavior, can be of concern, especially when outcomes from heavy usage are not deemed socially acceptable. Social media platforms for sharing user content (Facebook/Meta, Twitter, LinkedIn) as well as ride finding/sharing (Lyft, Uber), lodging finding (Airbnb, Travelocity), online shopping (Amazon, Walmart, Costco), online selling (eBay), and online apps for mobile devices, including music, video, and other streaming services (Apple, Google, Netflix), speak to the proliferation of platforms in these early stages. The types of AI that underlie these use cases vary, but most often include AI-based recommendation systems for customers. A *recommendation system* suggests what a customer might want to buy. The list of platform businesses has grown rapidly in the last decade since the invention of smartphones. An especially interesting segment includes platforms that provide earning opportunities for others on their platforms.

The platform society is envisioned as a way for individuals to earn a portion of their livelihood as part of a support economy that blurs the line between employees, customers, and partners. Both platform providers and platform earners are trying to find ways to use AI to improve the ability to earn a living on the platform.

Labor platforms are those that require time and skills (e.g., Lyft drivers), and capital platforms are those that require assets, time, and skills (e.g., eBay sellers). By focusing on skills, both providers and earners see opportunities for AI systems to automate and augment. In fact, AI provides a way for labor platforms to become capital platforms for earners.

How can AI help responsible labor platforms transform into capital platforms for earners? For example, Lyft the platform could potentially improve profitability with robot drivers (automate); Lyft the drivers/earners could potentially increase earnings by buying and leasing tele-robotic cars to Lyft so that Lyft does not have to own assets (augment). Because of both technical and social barriers, fully robot-driver/driverless vehicles are unlikely to be accepted for some time, creating tele-robotic opportunities for one earner to be operating multiple vehicles simultaneously. Earners on platforms foresee a franchise owner possibility in the future as AI capabilities improve. In the late 1800s, Singer ensured that customers could buy his sewing machines with a very small down payment and pay the rest over time, because he realized owners of sewing machines would be able to increase their income by sewing for neighbors and create the income stream they needed to make the purchase. The same may be true of most labor platforms in the future, as AI augments earners and responsible platform owners invest in AI to automate (major portions of the skilled work that earners perform). Of course, there is the fear that platform owners might want to take all the profits via complete automation —but governments may step in if that is the case.

AI can also help responsible capital platforms transform to improve earner's ability to earn. For example, eBay the platform could provide robot *junk* remover service for homes. While these capabilities are well beyond service robots today, the capabilities may eventually exist, if there is an ROI. Again, like the Singer sewing machine example, by empowering earners to provide the service in their regions, a franchise model could be developed for eBay and other responsible capital platforms that want to empower their earners. Ultimately, it is the *enlightened self-interest* of platform owners, businesses, and governments, to eliminate poverty traps, and ensure both earning and spending drive investing for retirement and wealth creation for all stakeholders. Henry Ford realized this when he made owning a car a realistic goal for his employees by paying them a fair wage.

CHAPTER 3

Questions

As AI solves the problem of scaling service, via automation and augmentation, venture capitalists, businesses, and governments will be making further massive investments to improve AI capabilities in the coming decades. Next, we present some challenging questions for you to consider. For hints about approaches to answering these questions, see the endnotes section of this book. Before looking at the hints, think about how you would go about answering each of these questions yourself—or come up with questions of your own about the future of service in the AI era.

For practitioners, who are all workers in general, how will AI automation and augmentation impact the future of work for both high-skill and routine types of work? Can AI help business and government leaders better predict future costs of service? CEOs ask AI experts "when will an AI capability be available at a particular annualized cost?" This type of information is key to planning for the future. For example, today, in 2022, to hire an excellent data scientist in Silicon Valley California, the cost would be about $300K per year. Some predict that by 2040, an excellent digital worker (AI-powered) data scientist will cost about $100K per year. How would you go about answering this type of question in general? Would you be thinking of replacing people with machines (automation), or would you be thinking of hiring people who really know how to use AI well (augmentation), or both? What kind of leader of machines or people would you be as CEO? What is the purpose of human resources (HR) departments in the AI era?

For educators, who work with learners, how will AI automation and augmentation impact the future of education, including how much and how quickly we can learn, and to what purposes people can apply what they know? Is there a role for AI in helping people to unlearn what is no longer of value? For example, those familiar with Apple's *Knowledge Navigator* video may see one answer to the augmentation questions, as they envision AI-powered graduate students, post-docs, and teaching assistants to empower faculty to get more or different types of research done in new ways. Some other questions for educators: Will disciplines remain stable in the era of AI? What new disciplines will emerge? Which existing disciplines will have sub-specializations forming? Will disciplines begin merging in some fashion? What will AI-empowered faculty, students, universities, and academic disciplines look like? Educators work especially hard to help the next generation of learners and are often viewed as experts in narrow areas of knowledge. How is this likely to change in the AI era?

For scholars, how will AI automation and augmentation accelerate scientific discoveries? What might be some unintended consequences? The three key constraints of being human—limited lifespan (physical), learning rate (mental), and social network sizes (social)—may suggest areas for new discoveries if these constraints were to be extended by an order of magnitude (10 times better) via AI technologies. As our lifetime of experiences (our personal datasets) become transformed into more advanced AI system, will a type of virtual immortality be possible? Will scholars augmented by AI continue to strive to answer research questions in their narrow discipline, or will they develop new methodologies and approaches to determine in new and better ways, exactly which questions to try to answer? Leading scholars build research centers about the same size as startup companies to answer questions, so is it likely that leading scholars will build even larger AI-enabled research centers to pursue questions previously unimaginably ambitious? How will industry–university–government collaborations evolve in the AI era?

PART II

Science

All models are wrong, some are useful.

—George Box

Nothing in life is to be feared, it is only to be understood. Now is the time to understand more, so that we may fear less.
—Marie Curie, as quoted in *Our Precarious Habitat* (1973) by Melvin A. Benarde

Any sufficiently advanced technology is indistinguishable from magic.
—Arthur C. Clark, 1985, *Profiles of the Future*, "Hazards of Prophecy"

Science in the service of humanity is technology, but lack of wisdom may make the service harmful.
—Isaac Asimov, 1988, in Epigraph of Isaac Asmiov's *Book of Science and Nature Quotations*

...though the world does not change with a change of paradigm, the scientist afterward works in a different world... What man sees depends both upon what he looks at and also upon what his previous visual-conception experience has taught him to see...
—Thomas S. Kuhn, 1962, in *The Structure of Scientific Revolutions*

We live in an increasing complex and interconnected world that contains more and more large complex systems. Operations of large complex systems requires teams of managers with good working relations and overlapping skills. To prepare students for such a world by enculturating them in emic disciplinary views with no countervailing overview is mis-training. We elders have an obligation to provide the upcoming generation with overviews that are simultaneously under-standable, realistic, forward-looking, and whole. I will call this "the obligation of the elders."

—Stephen J. Kline, 1995, in *Conceptual Foundations of Multidisciplinary Thinking*

CHAPTER 4

Foundations of the Sciences

Scientists study the world and build models. Broadly speaking, scientists study phenomena that fall into three realms: Natural sciences (physics, chemistry, biology, earth sciences, ecology, etc.), social sciences (anthropology, economics, cognitive science, history, etc.), and formal sciences (mathematics, computer science, etc.). *Each of the sciences studies a different type of system*, possibly at different scales, using a mixture of quantitative and qualitative methods to build models. For example, quantitative methods include building a mathematical model of a part of the world (e.g., in physics, Einstein's $E = mc^2$), whereas qualitative methods, including mapping and organizing types of observed variety into models (e.g., in chemistry, Mendeleev's Periodic Table of Elements); in practice, all sciences use a mixture of quantitative and qualitative methods to build models. *All sciences develop methods of measuring phenomena to evaluate the quality of their models as successively better explanations for observed categories of data of some aspect of the world.* AI is an especially interesting area of scientific study, because it touches on all three types of sciences and is therefore *transdisciplinary.* AI runs on hardware which depends on physics (natural sciences), the evaluation of AI requires modeling cognitive tasks (social sciences), and AI itself is considered part of computer science (formal sciences).

The purest purpose of the sciences is to build better models. *Models are a kind of knowledge used to explain the systems of the world more clearly and concisely.* The value of the sciences relates to the value of new knowledge in action. The application of knowledge can generate value for people. Business and societal value requires that the new knowledge be put in practice, which is the role of practitioners. New knowledge can lead to service innovations that change interactions for the better; specifically, investment in science (university scholars, industry research and development (R&D), government policy analysts) may create new knowledge to improve service productivity, quality, regulatory compliance, and more. Some economists see a virtuous circle between science and service. Especially economists who think about the economy as sectors and see R&D as part of the data-driven, science-based, high-value service sector.

Trust is key in both science and service. Confidence in new knowledge produced by people applying the scientific method (experiments that test hypotheses) is increased by two factors: openness and reproducibility. In theory, anyone with the ability to read can get access to scientific publications (openness) and replicate the experiment (reproducibility). In practice, the cost of accessing scientific journals and the necessary laboratory equipment is prohibitive, except for a few. Nations and businesses compete to *out science* each other. Again, this gap between the ideal of democratic, trusted science, and the high table-stakes of science today speaks directly to the need for innovation and improvement in science as a democratized and trusted service.

CHAPTER 5

Service Science

Look out at the natural world. Plants and animals form an evolving ecology (a model of change and interaction). Populations of organisms interact in fantastically complex ways. All the organisms you see today are built from cells that contain DNA, which has been evolving for several billion years. The scientists who are known as biologists study an evolving ecology of DNA-based living entities. You can thank biologists for building models of the world that have helped save countless lives.

An Evolving Ecology

The community of practice known as the service research community includes people who contribute to advancing the study of service science. When biologists look at that world, they see living things, but when service scientists look at the world, they see more. Service scientists look at the world and see social, economic, and political actors (people, businesses, nations, and other types of responsible actors) interacting in wonderfully complex ways. Service scientists see people with different skills, businesses in different industry sectors, nations with different cultures and rule systems. This service ecology is in fact made up of service systems with names and identities. Often, they have an aspiration about their future. For example, IBM wants to be a better version of itself in the future; each of us, Jim, Paul, Steve, and Markus, wants to be a better version of ourselves in the future; the United States, a nation, wants to be a better version of itself in the future—or at least certain leaders and citizens want that to be true. So, we define identity in terms of today's capabilities as well as future aspirations. *Responsible actors are named legal entities.* They can own resources as property, sign contractual agreements, and be taken to court if they violate the terms of those agreements. Responsible actors have reputations. Their reputations are determined in part by the outcomes of their interactions with others.

Responsible actors are in a process of becoming future versions of themselves. Service scientists study an evolving ecology of responsible actors interconnected by value propositions; a model of change and interaction. Fundamental to service science is the fact that responsible actors have incentives to interact with trusted others, for example, interacting with family members. In business and government, things get a little trickier—because trusting strangers is a bigger leap. In jargon, the bigger leap is a *value proposition*. Populations of responsible actors are interacting with each other in service networks. Interactions happen through value propositions or promises to cooperate and to reconfigure access rights to resources that they possess or control. Different stakeholders may have different measures for how mutually beneficial win-win value propositions will be. Measures such as productivity, quality, compliance, and sustainable innovation all matter to different stakeholders; for example, government is an authority stakeholder, and authority stakeholders care about regulatory compliance of value propositions. Governments reserve for themselves the unique right to include coercion in their value propositions: pay your taxes or go to jail. People and businesses cannot use coercion (the threat of physical or psychological harm) in value propositions to the degree governments can. That is a huge difference between governments as responsible service system actors and other types of actors, such as people and businesses, interacting through value propositions or promises to cooperate in win-win games. To service scientists, all these differences between actors and their complex interactions are fascinating.

Great service outcomes are win-win outcomes: two responsible actors interact, with both gaining benefit (win-win outcomes). However, lose-win, win-lose, and lose-lose are also possibilities in two-player games. In fact, service scientists have described 10 possible outcomes for responsible actor interactions (including dispute resolution). Outcomes affect the reputation of actors. Reputation affects identity. Responsible actors compete for collaborators with varying degrees of success. When actors have a reputation for helping others, while simultaneously and fairly helping themselves, they are said to have a good reputation for value cocreation outcomes.

The knowledge used in nature's *interaction games* has been evolving in biological *neural nets, or more simply brains*, for about 500 million years (clams, tribolites, bees, etc.), in hominids for about two million years, and in specialized-work, city-dwelling, tool-builder people for about 20,000 years. If each generation is roughly 20 years, about 1,000 generations of humans have been accumulating knowledge, part of larger and larger responsible actors capable of configuring access rights to resources in more and more sophisticated knowledge-based value propositions. Service scientists find the evolving ecology of knowledge-based responsible actors (over 1,000 generations) as fascinating as biologists find the evolving ecology of DNA-based living entities (over trillions of generations of bacteria).

An Emerging Transdiscipline

Real-world problems do not respect academic discipline boundaries. Service science is an emerging transdiscipline. *A transdiscipline provides an integrative overview of a set of disciplines and the knowledge they organize, without replacing any of the component disciplines.* Or more simply, a transdiscipline tries to harness all other disciplines like a team of horses.

Academic disciplines organize the types of knowledge about the world across a broad spectrum, and industry sectors organize the types of knowledge about mutually beneficial interactions across a broad spectrum. Service scientists have proposed ways of organizing disciplines and industries. They have also encouraged the *notion of T-shaped skills, or breadth and depth (like the letter T, broad at the top and deep underneath).* A service scientist should have broad knowledge of all disciplines and all industries and be deep in one or more. For example, a professional might specialize in marketing applied to retail or computer science applied to health care. In addition to disciplines and industries, service scientists should also have a broad knowledge of service in many cultures and be deep in one or more cultural perspectives.

In sum, service science tries to harness all disciplines, natural, social, formal, and practical, like a team of horses pulling the load of better win-win interactions and change. Or in jargon, responsible actors reconfiguring access rights to resources in win-win interactions underlies the phenomenon of value cocreation, which is the essence of service interactions from a service science perspective. When win-win outcomes are achieved, the quantity of resources grows, as does the positive reputations of the responsible actors. Trust grows as reputations improve, which sets the stage for successfully competing for collaborators to create larger-scale responsible actors. Limiting the downside for responsible actors, when win-win is not achieved and disputes arise, allows actors to take on more risk, be more entrepreneurial, and explore more knowledge-value realms (disciplines, industries, cultures, etc.). Competition, conflict, and disputes can actually accelerate learning for a population of responsible actors by testing boundary cases and deepening mutual understanding (better models of each other's inner logics). As mentioned, beyond disciplines and industries, cultures and rule systems provide another knowledge-value realm to be explored. As an emerging transdiscipline, service science is less than twenty years old, and studies a phenomenon that has been evolving for about 1,000 generations of people, growing to include responsible actors such as businesses and nations.

To understand what is new about AI coming to service, consider this question: where is the knowledge that people use in their service interactions stored? For the earliest people, our brains as well as the natural and social environment can be viewed as knowledge repositories. Parents and peers are knowledge repositories. Educators are knowledge repositories. Next, for people with writing and reading capabilities, books became information repositories that could be *re-hydrated* so to speak, and transformed into knowledge when people read, understood, and applied their understanding. In the increasingly digital world of today, information is not only stored in digital books and videos, but increasingly in the form of AI models of the world for performing specific tasks. Books and videos could not apply the information inside them to do things, but properly connected AI models can act in the world. What is an AI model? *AI models are sometimes called neural networks.* They are a kind of quantitative, mathematical model that given an input, such as the picture of a rose, produces an output, the word *rose*.

Data science and AI can also be viewed as transdisciplines from the perspective that all disciplines will eventually have AI models and the datasets used to create them. So, in some sense, all disciplines with AI models are becoming transdisciplinary. However, the mutual benefits that responsible actors realize (cocreate) through the application of knowledge is where the focus of service science resides. This involves the actual entities, interactions, and outcomes of an evolving ecology of responsible actors learning to invest systematically in *better* future versions of themselves.

Does all this mean service science is *just* the study of the social world of people? So far, the responsible actors such as businesses and nations that are studied by service science, all include people. However, as other types of actors gain rights and responsibilities, the domain of service science will need to be expanded to include those entities as well. So far, AI systems cannot act responsibly, they do not have adequate cognitive capabilities, nor do they exist with any legal standing as responsible entities in the world. Only in science fictions, like the *Bicentennial Man* or Star Trek Next Generation, do we see humanoid AI systems seeking to be legally recognized as responsible actors (see the endnotes for a noteworthy exception to prove the rule).

CHAPTER 6

Questions

Science is both a process (way to do something) and communities of practice (disciplines) that build better models of the world, and service science seeks to harness all disciplines to build better models of service. Again, we present some challenging questions for you. Again, for hints about approaches to answering these questions, see the endnotes section of this book, but before looking at the hints, think about how you would go about answering these questions, or come up with questions of your own to answer about science, service science, and the future of science.

For practitioners, who are all workers in general, the question is how to set and achieve important goals more rigorously. How can practitioners with better models of the world deliver service offering the world most needs while growing a profitable business doing so? For example, the initial aspiration is often a more profitable business that delights more and more customers while also growing revenue and increasing shareholder value. From this perspective, the fundamental question is how to make better investment decisions to maximize the utility of resources at hand while trying to anticipate inevitable disruptions that may be lurking just over the horizon. While most business practitioners focus on scaling up, sometimes the focus should be on scaling down intelligently while transforming into something new and more adaptive. For example, scaling up typically means growing business revenues, but during a pandemic, scaling down or business survival may be a higher priority. When a responsible actor becomes a better (more adaptive) future version of itself, it is better able to cocreate value and to co-elevate capabilities with all the other diverse responsible actors in the environment. Is the most important goal in business survival or transformation, or something else? What if the most important goal in business was to help more people live a meaningful life with a shared worthy purpose? Businesses do provide the service of helping people (employees) develop and grow in their career, while simultaneously helping many customers. In what ways does a platform in the era of AI begin to erase the distinction between employee and customer? What is the role of the leader and human resources (HR) as the science of responsible entities learning to invest in becoming better future versions of themselves advances?

Of the many possible questions to ask practitioners, one of the most important in the era of AI is how can businesses become more data-driven, like a science, doing the right trials (scientific experiments) at the right time? What are the business processes of the past and today? What evolutionary trajectory are the business processes on? Is the business (as a service system responsible actor) becoming a better future version of itself? Is the business scaling up (growing/surviving) or scaling down (morphing/transforming) intelligently? How can AI and other techniques help break the trade-off between efficient service and customized service? How can AI and other techniques help businesses compete for collaborators (customers, employees, partners, etc.)? How can AI help business platforms, erase the difference between customer, employee, and partner and help all who participate in the platform become better (l)earners—upskilling learners who earn (profit) while simultaneously using and improving the platform? What can be done to better align individuals, organizations (including government institutions), infrastructure, and information that leads to wiser decision making as judged by future generations?

For educators, there have been numerous advances in teaching about service from a disciplinary perspective (e.g., marketing, operations management, systems engineering, design, computing and cloud, economics, information systems) but less progress in a creating a truly transdisciplinary approach to educating the next generation about service science. So one important question for educators is how can a better transdisciplinary approach be created? For example, in the AI era, digital twins (AI models of resources) are being created for all types of resources that exist in service networks, including digital twins for responsible actors (e.g., people, businesses, governments). Would teaching students about digital twins—as well as complexity economics (agent-based simulation models of entities with adaptive strategies for interacting, including playing win-win games)—be the best starting point for teaching students about the *whole* transdiscipline of service science? Does service science say anything about the evolution of jobs? How will the service that educators provide evolve in the AI era when influence becomes as important as expertise? In the AI era, will educators develop value propositions that help them more directly benefit from the future success of their students?

For scholars, from a service science perspective, trust in scientific knowledge is a complex and urgent grand challenge. The primary question is often how best to discover and openly share new important and relevant knowledge. The negative consequences of a population that does not have a common understanding of science and the technologies and policies built on that scientific foundation is already beginning to be experienced in highly advanced nations today. How might scholars reinvent both notions of scientific progress (building models of the world that provide better explanations and more utility to people, including under-served populations) as well as the service they provide to society in the AI era?

In sum, better trials, transdisciplinarity, and trust are three promising roads ahead for service science to advance in the era of AI.

PART III

Logic

The greatest danger in times of turbulence is not the turbulence: it is to act with yesterday's logic.

—Peter F. Drucker

Without changing our pattern of thought, we will not be able to solve the problems we created with our current pattern of thought.

—Albert Einstein

We do not see things as they are. We see things as we are.

—Anais Nin

The main power base of paradigms may be in the fact that they are taken for granted and not explicitly questioned.

—Johan Arndt

CHAPTER 7

Foundations of Logics and Dominant Logics

A *logic* is a conceptual lens for observing the world and understanding how it works. It is also sometimes referred to as a *mental model* or a *paradigm*. Those who use the same logic have a shared mindset for reasoning about the world and for making decisions and taking actions. Logics are very powerful, partly because you are usually unaware that you are using them.

Because science is based on observations of the world, a logic is a key part of the philosophical foundations of any science. In fact, logics often originate in scientific thinking. The most common logic of science is *Newtonian mechanics*. It describes the world in terms of macroscopic objects with *innate properties* that have causative powers, such as the gravitational force of the earth. Therefore, it sees the role of science as discovering and describing the predictable relationships among these properties, which form the basis of theory about the behavior of objects—that is, physics. It is a very powerful logic that has widespread influence, beyond physics, to other sciences, such as economics, as well as to non-scientific understandings, like how you understand our relationships with other people (e.g., "s/he made me do it").

However, Newtonian mechanics is not the only scientific logic. Increasingly, a newer logic is gradually becoming seen as providing a more fundamental understanding of the world than Newtonian mechanics: the logic of *quantum mechanics*. Quantum mechanics describes the world in terms of microscopic objects, which are too small to be part of ordinary human experience, such as atoms and subatomic particles. In quantum mechanics, the nature and properties of objects are not fixed but vary, depending on their context and interaction with other objects. Rather than predictable, it sees the world as probabilistic and, rather than deterministic relationships, it sees the world in terms of systemic relationships.

Logics can be compared based on size and coverage. Size refers to the number of concepts (words with specific meanings) and sentences (that connect the concepts into meaningful wholes). Coverage refers to how much of the world can be described and explained. The principle of parsimony prefers maximum coverage from minimum size. Sentences are often referred to as propositions, and when reduced to their smallest number, they are called axioms—those from which all other propositions can be derived.

A logic is dominant if it is the prevailing logic that is used by a community of practice, implicitly as a bias or explicitly as a social practice. A dominant or common logic can help create a shared understanding of events by community members. This is *enabling* because it affords cooperation and the coordination of activities. However, it can also be *constraining*, because it restricts vision, often because of *confirmation bias*—seeing what is expected. Some logics, such as Newtonian mechanics, are so dominant that they are adopted across communities and impact views of how almost everything in the world works. Once dominant, partly due to confirmation bias, logics tend to be resilient and difficult to change. However, even very entrenched dominant logics can change over time. For example, thinking the earth is flat or that the sun goes around the earth were once dominant logics but have now been pretty much abandoned or, more accurately, displaced by a newer logic. This movement from one logic to another is known as a *paradigm shift* and can be a decades-long process. Often, though not always, paradigm shifts begin in scientific thinking when it becomes apparent that the old logic has become inadequate for explaining relevant phenomena.

CHAPTER 8

Service-Dominant Logic

The dominance of Newtonian mechanics can be seen in how you think about business, economics, and marketing, in addition to physics. It has resulted in a mental model of economic activity in terms of things (i.e., products/goods) embedded with properties (e.g., value, utility), sometimes referred to as *goods-dominant (G-D) logic*. Consider how you typically think about an economic exchange: buying a new car with cash. According to G-D logic, cash has value, a new car has value, and buying a new car for cash would be seen as an exchange of money for goods. It does not matter where the cash came from, where the car came from, or what uses these will be put to after the exchange. It is just seen as (embedded) *value-for-value* exchange, albeit moderated by price, based on supply and demand, which are themselves properties of the market.

Service-for-Service Exchange and Value

Now, an alternative logic is emerging, one that takes a broader view of the context and role of economic exchange in society to try to understand how *value is cocreated through systems of exchange*. This alternative logic has been called *service-dominant (S-D) logic*, because it maintains that this exchange is better understood in terms of *service-for-service* than in terms of goods-for-goods or goods-for-money (value-for-value). That is, it is about the *process* and *outcome* of actors (e.g., people and organizations) applying their resources, such as knowledge, for the benefit of others— that is, *service provision*—in exchange for others providing service for them. In S-D logic, rather than something that is embedded, value is an outcome, a change in the well-being of the focal system (individual/ organization).

More precisely, S-D logic is based on five specific propositions: (axioms): (a) service is the basis of exchange, (b) value is always cocreated by a multitude of actors, (c) actors obtain new resources through the integration of resources obtained through service exchange, (d) value is a measure of the well-being of a focal beneficiary, and (e) institutions (e.g., social norms, rules, norms) play an important role in the coordination of direct and indirect value cocreation. The implications of these propositions can be nuanced and may be difficult to accept by those entrenched in the traditional G-D logic mindset, in which things (rather than actions and outcomes) are the key concepts.

Consider how the car-buying situation would be viewed from an S-D logic perspective. Rather than a value-for-value (car-for-money exchange), it would be seen as a service-for-service exchange, but that is just an interim event—that is, "I'll do something for you if you will do something for me." Rather than the car having the property of embedded value, it would be seen as only having potential value to the buyer, to be realized, in context, through its integration with additional (potential) resources, such as knowledge of driving, access to petroleum, use of a highway system, and so on. Likewise, the cash only represents potential value for the seller. That is, *money represents rights to future service*, from which value can only be realized fully through the integration of resources obtained with other resources available to the buyer. Furthermore, both the car and the money being exchanged came about through prior, complex resource integration and service exchange activities, often involving thousands, if not millions of people.

Service Ecosystems and Knowledge-Driven Value Cocreation

In short, S-D logic sees value creation as an interactive (direct and indirect), continual, widely distributed process, taking place in *service ecosystems*. These service ecosystems are coordinated through shared mental models—that is, their own dominant logics—which additionally provide the standards for judging what is valuable and what is not—that is, the *values* used in the evaluation of the outcomes (value) of service provision and resource integration. All of this implies the importance of understanding that value creation is knowledge driven, distributed, and intertwined. It means shifting primary attention away from making things to designing service ecosystems for mutual benefit.

G-D logic does not provide much insight into the potential role of or most beneficial use of AI. Essentially, it is just seen as another technology to be sold, albeit one that can act on the humans that invented it. On the other hand, S-D logic provides a powerful mindset for considering AI's potential role in mutual value creation, through the expansion of resource integration and service exchange in service ecosystems. It also affords participation in ecosystems design and management. Many scholars, educators, and practitioners will continue to use G-D logic, until the powerful mindset benefits of S-D logic become explicit or are implicitly adopted.

CHAPTER 9

Questions

Logics and dominant logics, including S-D logic, are now introduced. Those who embrace S-D logic can more clearly see the world of service-for-service exchange that surrounds them and of which they are a part, as well as the nature of knowledge-driven value cocreation in ecosystems. Again, we present some challenging questions for you. For hints about approaches to answering these questions, see the notes section of this book, but before looking at the hints, think about how you would go about answering each of these questions, or come up with questions of your own to answer about S-D logic.

For practitioners, who are all workers in general, how does using S-D logic provide advantages over G-D logic when thinking about the adoption of AI technologies in business and government?

For educators, who work with learners, how can teaching of new logics be accelerated into society? Solving the most challenging problems often requires being able to look at the problems from multiple perspectives.

For scholars, how can adopting S-D logic lead to new discoveries that advance business and society? For example, economists measuring economic activity with G-D logic, which originated when the economy was dominated by agricultural and early manufacturing activities, may gain new insights now that the knowledge- and AI-intensive activities are becoming a larger proportion of overall interactions.

PART IV

Architecture

Enterprise architecture is the organizing logic for business processes and IT infrastructure, reflecting the integration and standardization requirements of the company's operating model.

—Jeanne W. Ross

If you want truly to understand something, try to change it.

—Kurt Lewin

As an architect you design for the present, with an awareness of the past, for a future which is essentially unknown.

—Norman Foster

Design is the conscious and intuitive effort to impose meaningful order.

—Victor Papanek

Moving up a level in generality, I tried to understand the broader institutional regularities among the systems that were sustained over a long period of time and were absent in the failed systems. I used the term "design principle" to characterize these regularities ... the design principles appear to synthesize core factors that affect the probability of long-term survival of an institution developed by the users of a resource.

—Eleanor Ostrom, Nobel Prize Acceptance Speech

...each pattern represents our current best guess as to what arrangement of the physical environment will work to solve the problem presented.

—Christopher Alexander

The Bauhaus was the starting point of a comprehensive understanding of design that is in even greater demand today. With terms such as social design, open design and design thinking, the discussion of how designers can see their work in a broader context and thereby contribute to shaping society has begun anew.

—Mateo Kries

Structuralism asserts a logical primacy of the whole over the parts and attempts to grasp an inner connection of the phenomena as a structure.

—Roman Jakobson

Duality of structure—structure as the medium and outcome of the conduct it recursively organizes.

—Anthony Giddens

CHAPTER 10

Foundations of Architectures and Dominant Architectures

What is architecture, and why does it matter? Over the past 20,000 years (a thousand generations)—since the early cities with specialized skills and roles—the architecture of buildings, organizations, and technologies has been changing. Most people are familiar with the architecture of buildings, but organizations have architectures as well. For example, historically, empires relied on coercion and trade to grow the scope and scale of their operations and holdings, meaning the design pattern of their *organizational architecture* or *enterprise architecture* included both military and supply chains distributed across an interconnected network of cities. The architecture of cities and places where you live and work affects the ease of getting things done and your quality of life and your well-being. Homes, cities, and organizations (as enterprises)—places of work, learning, health care, and so on—are the places you spend the most time and are designed to support your daily activities.

Making Simple Changes Easy and Hard Changes Possible

Good architectures make simple changes easy (e.g., rearranging furniture) and hard changes possible (e.g., moving a wall with plumbing and electrical). If nothing much changed in human activities, architecture would be easier. But every society, every city, and every enterprise is in a state of perpetual change, a process of becoming, striving to become a better future version of itself. The primary reason that enterprise architecture matters is because some architectures allow the needed change to improve service functions more easily than others. As technologies and strategies change, the demands on enterprise architecture are increasing. Openness to collaboration, rules for coordinating actors in actor-to-actor networks, and skills such as integrating and orchestrating external resources are required.

In the era of artificial intelligence (AI), good enterprise architecture allows new offerings (customer solutions) to be created and changed rapidly and with flexibility in how datasets are used to drive business growth. Data-driven insights trigger tactical or strategic business moves and data-driven network effects. This results in further requirements for the enterprise architecture and in particular for the patterns of how data are collected, analyzed, and used in context.

How Architectures Become Dominant Architectures

What is a dominant architecture? As in the previous chapter, *dominant* refers to how many people adopt and embrace a particular mindset and worldview, including both users (practitioners) and influencers (scholars and educators). Architecture can, therefore, be called dominant when its design patterns for change become part of social and cultural practices and are reused over and over again in different social, organizational, and technological contexts.

Here, we focus on *enterprise architecture*. Put simply, the architecture of a building includes interconnected room structures (floor plan) that provide service, and *the architecture of an enterprise includes interconnected organization functions (organization plan) that provide service*. Economic actors are in a race to find the best enterprise architecture. The race is on to become the dominant architecture that can best support the required changes, constantly adapting to multiple environmental factors (e.g., competitors, regulations, technologies, customer preferences, employees, partners, shareholders, etc.) while competing for collaborators.

CHAPTER 11

Service Dominant Architecture

About only a 100 years ago (five generations of people), the modern corporation arose. Recently, in the era of digital transformations, the rise of platform companies, such as Airbnb and Uber, are giving a new meaning to traditional notions of return on assets. With the divorce of ownership from control, a new design pattern for management and governance—and by means of these—a new design for enterprise architecture emerged. By facilitating continuity regardless of the succession plan and opening up new forms of financing, the pattern is being actively reused across industry sectors and is still rapidly evolving today.

Emergence of Service-Oriented Architecture

About 60 years ago (three generations of people), computer programming languages like COBOL were designed for enterprise business use. The power of mainframe computers with large-scale batch and transaction processing made possible the integration and operation of more and more applications that incorporate business knowledge. In this way, business processes, such as accounting, controlling, or personnel planning, were gradually transferred from humans to machines. The downside of decades of integration, expansion, and further development is the emergence of monolithic applications and monolithic enterprise architectures, characterized by high complexity and dependencies of interwoven programs, by head monopolies of few employees, by accompanying closedness, high maintenance requirements, and slowness resulting from long release cycles.

In the late 1990s, service-oriented architecture (SOA) emerged as a paradigm for organizing and using shared modular service capabilities to enable modularity, flexibility, and openness. SOA service modules are built in a way that represents repeatable business activities. The underlying SOA design pattern always consists of the three roles of service provider, service broker, and service customer. Combined with principles, such as loose coupling, compatibility, and reusability of the service module, it became possible to create component-based applications with high interoperability and without technology lock-in. In this way, SOA enables organizational benefits, such as openness to the use of service modules outside the enterprise, speed, scalability, and cost advantages. The SOA enterprise architecture has evolved significantly over the last 20 years (one generation) with improved governance and maturity models.

Emergence of Digital Attacker Platform Architecture

Today, traditional industries are under attack by digital rivals (such as Airbnb, Uber, and even Amazon) with business models and business operations based entirely on digital platforms. Despite the growing sophistication of traditional enterprise architecture, such as the SOA enterprise architecture, they are still being disrupted, as they do not allow fast-enough change against digital attackers.

Based on cloud technologies and open-source software platforms, companies do not have to install and operate software on their own. Software, infrastructure, and even whole technological platform stacks offered as microservices facilitate the emergence of platform companies based on the pattern of openness and connectivity. Platform companies are characterized by five roles: platform owner, platform provider, value proposition provider, complementor, and beneficiary. The strength of these digital platform architectures is to enable these roles by bringing together resources and data at breathtaking speed. Combined with low copying costs, digital platforms aggregate digital resources and thus build up an immensely high resource density—not simply more transistor per unit area on chips, but more interconnected fast-changing components from more vendors orchestrated more easily. And with it, the opportunities for the next attackers who will define the rules of the race by bringing the design pattern to act on this resource density to the table.

Emergence of Service Dominant Architecture

Service Dominant Architecture (SDA) is grounded in service-dominant (S-D) logic and service science and provides an organizing logic for shaping companies, service platforms, and service ecosystems through design patterns aimed at making it possible to build and orchestrate capabilities in a systematic way. SDA allows for rapid change and adoption of new technologies, including AI, to accelerate digital transformation and to turn resource density into true, market-accelerating service innovations. The goal is to make businesses better—more agile, more sense-and-respond, better able to keep up with and drive meaningful human-centered change in a fast-paced world, while also maintaining privacy, security, and regulatory compliance.

Based on platform technologies, SDA is a set of design patterns that enables responsible actors (e.g., individuals, companies, and organizations) to act in the context of openness and connectivity in a meaningful way and to organize service as a transdisciplinary process of value cocreation. SDA provides a transcending perspective on enterprise architecture by reimagining the enterprise in the terms of S-D logic, supporting five specific roles: (1) sense-and-respond cocreation interactions with actors (e.g., customers), (2) frictionless onboarding and participation of partners, (3) rapid integration of operant resources (including employees), (4) improved insights from data for all stakeholders, and (5) actor coordination by institutions as rules and norms (service catalog).

Consider again the example of buying a car. SDA's roles allow it to onboard other partners such as telematics providers to collaborate on personalized value propositions, such as changing tires or picking up to inspect the vehicle based on driving behavior. Integrating the resources of more and more partners enables new combinatorial opportunities and value propositions that cover the entire spectrum of mobility, such as car sharing, bike rental, e-scooters. The customer interacts to benefit from the application of the capabilities offered by continually improving value propositions. In this process, resources are integrated, and service is exchanged for service. With each transaction, all stakeholder data are updated in the data lake (set of operational data stores), leading to improved insights with the help of AI. This enables win-win-win relationships; on the one hand between car sellers and buyers with constantly improving mobility offers, and on the other hand, the data and the insights gained from it benefit the entire network.

The technical implementation of SDA can be compared to Lego. Open-source and cloud platform technologies form the base plate. Technical, functional, and business services are implemented as generic or specific bricks. Each brick is preconfigured with the five roles as systems. The base plate and the bricks are coordinated via the SDA service catalog that sets the rules and standards.

Once the bricks (technology systems consisting of microservices) are used by actors (service system), the process of actor engagement and value cocreation is organized and structured. After value is delivered in one system (e.g., by accumulating data), the system drives value for other SDA systems. For example, data are fed into the data lake (facilitating data analytics), advanced forms of collaboration between human and technological actors—such as, workforce management as combinations of employer + AI, employee + AI, technology + AI—are enabled, capabilities become exchangeable and tradeable via the service catalog, and resource density is built. Thus, SDA facilitates the reshaping of operating architectures of enterprises, service platforms, service ecosystems, and markets by making simple changes (e.g., digital solutions as value propositions) easy and hard changes (e.g., digital transformation and platform organizations) possible.

In a world of constant change and transformation, it is important to understand the ways that good architecture can make simple changes easy, and complex changes possible. While actor-to-actor networks spread and new connections are made, the density of resources and capabilities increases, and with it, the need for enterprises and other organizations to have a construction plan for reshaping the operating architecture. SDA is an emerging architecture based on S-D logic and service science that aims to clarify what enterprises should consider to better reshape their operating model to be prepared for continuous upskilling (e.g., by exploiting AI) and to engage in the process of value cocreation.

CHAPTER 12

Questions

Architecture and dominant architectures, as well as SDA, are now introduced. Again, we present some challenging questions for you. As done earlier, for hints about approaches to answering these questions, see the endnotes section of this book, but before looking at the hints, think about how you would go about answering each of these questions, or come up with questions of your own to answer about SDA.

For practitioners, who are all workers in general, the challenge is growing a business based on adopting improved architectures (structures) and processes (new ways of doing things). What does *day 1* look like for a practitioner embracing SDA, at a startup or a large enterprise?

For educators, who work with learners, the challenge is teaching about the benefits of improved architectures. What does a textbook look like? How do you involve others when learners experiment with new types of service? What does an SDA lab look like, and how to involve open-source software development?

For scholars, the challenge is making new and significant discoveries related to architectures. What is the relationship between SDA and complexity economics—responsible actors adapting strategies? What will future dominant architectures be like, going even beyond SDA and the platform era? What new science and dominant logic will underlie the rules of the game, the competition to better combine and increase the density of capabilities easily available in more places? What will the attackers be like, forcing the change? Or, will *the game* be even more radically changed than we can imagine today? Will the very concepts of cooperation and competition be considered quaint, and remnants of a time of inefficient and dangerous wandering of a primitive self-centered species? What big choices will responsible actors face when they decide to interact to change the world, and for what purposes?

Service in the AI Era Revisited

In this section, we present a vision of service in the AI era, which can be summarized as *X+AI*. X could be a person. X could be a car or an airplane. X could be a business or even a nation. X could be a community of practice associated with an academic discipline. The *+AI* part includes an AI model of X. Recall that AI models are sometimes called *neural networks*. They are a kind of quantitative, mathematical model that given an input, such as the picture of a rose, produces an output, the word *rose*. Some might call the *+AI* part the *digital twin* of X.

Goods-dominant (G-D) logic is how most people still look at the world, where X represents things, like a car or airplane; often physical things that can be bought and owned. Service science, service-dominant (S-D) logic, and Service Dominant Architecture (SDA) provide an alternative way of looking at the *X+AI* world that is emerging. X can be viewed as an actor, and the capabilities of X can be accessed. Service science, S-D logic, and SDA provide a view of X and X+AI within the context of service, the application of resources (e.g., knowledge) for the benefit of another. One important benefit of this view is that access to information is a more general concept than ownership of physical things.

Better models of the world, better logics, and better architectures must ultimately be put to the test actor by actor, interaction by interaction, outcome by outcome, change by change. Interactions between actors can be viewed in terms of service-for-service exchange. Advances in science, technology, skills of people (*upskilling*), enterprise architecture, and even institutions can lead to innovations in interactions and changes to the world that benefit more and more stakeholders with win-win outcomes.

The X+AI Vision: Your Digital Service Twin

X+AI is still largely a vision because of gaps in AI capability. AI models as *neural nets* are as limiting as people modeled as brains. Models are useful simplification of a more complex system that exists in the world. Rethinking service in the AI era requires science, logic, and architecture perspective, if we are to create *better models* of the world (science), in people's minds (logics), and in the structure of business and government enterprises (architectures).

Despite the gaps in AI capabilities, the progression of AI in service as tool, assistant, collaborator, coach, and mediator seems to be happening. Writing this book, we have used AI tools such as spell checking and grammar checking. From AI search to translation, AI can be of assistance to authors as well. As collaborators, we have debated each other, while fully aware that debating technology and writing-completion technology are getting better. Online research platforms build models of users and provide coaching recommendations on books and articles to aid researchers. Nevertheless, there is still a huge gap in both AI capabilities and our trust of AI systems—a gap that must be closed before we can imagine an AI that knows us well enough to negotiate in service interactions on our behalf as a mediator, such as collaborating while writing a book or signing a contract on our behalf.

The X+AI model includes an AI model of you, *your digital service twin.* Your data is becoming your AI. Platform businesses use a digital twin they create of you and others to predict and personalize service offerings to appeal to you. Eventually, you will be able to use your own digital twin in many ways. In the X+AI vision, your digital service twin will help you do more, learn faster, and maybe interact with hundreds of people in parallel, even while you sleep. Your digital twin might continue some of your work even after you die. However, much can and will still go wrong. Misinformation often spreads faster than the truth. What happens to a brain/mind overwhelmed by misinformation? What can happen to a personal digital service twin if overwhelmed by misinformation? What if our digital service twin is hacked? And yet, for everyone with a smartphone, it is increasingly possible to imagine their apps *growing up* to become digital workers. What would you do if you had 100 digital workers working for you?

What Are Some Gaps Between Reality and Vision?

What is the reality of today's early-state AI? Four areas of rapid progress in the last 10 years are:

Memory capacity and search: IBM's Watson stored the equivalent of *Wikipedia and could easily retrieve all the articles with specific keywords. Most people cannot do that. Searching for information needed by scholars, educators and practitioners has never been easier.*

Pattern recognition and translation: Today's smartphone apps connected to the cloud can analyze a picture of a plant or animal and can easily retrieve what it likely is. Smartphone apps are also good a converting written or spoken speech in many languages to text, especially recognizing short questions or instructions (e.g., "What is the weather like?" or "Play a Beatle's song."). Translating between human languages is also getting good enough for many applications.

Recommendations and predictions: Thanks in part to AI techniques, computer systems have gotten very good at recommending: "if you like X, then you might also like Y." This is true from buying books, movies, music, as well as social media content on platforms. Platform owners are getting better at predicting what will keep people using their platform more intensely and for longer periods. Combined with pattern recognition, memory capacity and search, computer systems are also starting to help doctors provide better diagnosis, investors make investments, manufacturers and farmers weed out defective products.

Optimization and deductive reasoning: Where a problem can be represented as millions, billions, and even trillions of mathematical and quantitative constraints of a particular form, computer systems can solve for the best solution. Certain games, such as Chess and Go, can be formulated as mathematical optimization problems, or even robots learning to walk or manipulate objects in worlds simple enough to be robustly simulated. However, the complexity of the real world, especially when people are present (e.g., driverless vehicles), creates additional challenges.

The two big gaps for AI to be truly useful in daily service situations are:

Social learning: Not surprisingly, the one super-power of people is social learning ability. No other animal, not even chimpanzees, can match the human ability to learn by watching and listening to others, *imitating, and getting feedback in everyday social contexts. Children learn from their family and peers at a prodigious rate, and no AI system comes close today. Some scholars point to the nature of human dynamic episodic memory and what is called a theory of the mind. Humans have basic biological needs as well as complex goals and learn to point and follow eye gaze and wonder about what other people around them are thinking. Children's early episodic memories of their own hidden thoughts and the hidden thoughts of those around them perhaps mark the beginning of a theory of the mind. Human-like episodic memory is a model of the world, goals, plans, and a theory of mind. Today's early-stage AI systems do not yet have human-like episodic memories.*

Responsible learning: The transition from child to adult in human societies is marked by many rituals. Understanding service—the application of resources (e.g., knowledge) for the benefit of another—is the key to responsible learning. From families, to religions, to philosophies, to communities of practice and government institutions, people are shaped into responsible learners with a model of responsible learning. People not only have a model of their own mind and minds of others, but also have a model of what it means to be aware of what helps and harms others, what creates mutual benefits, and what does not, what is expected of others in family and societal roles. AI systems do not yet have a model of exchanging competences connected to responsible learning that allows filling roles responsibly in adult human society.

How long might it take to close these two big gaps? By around 2060, it might be possible to buy a device capable of performing a billion-billion calculations per second for $1,000. The human brain is estimated to perform this many calculations per second.

Let's explore what could go wrong with service in the X+AI era:

Dumbing down—I don't trust "myself": What if better service leads to downskilling rather than upskilling? People can become overly reliant on any technology to their own detriment. Food is a technology that has been improved greatly over the years, yet better food can lead to more obesity. Smarter systems can lead to less capable people. Investing in only making it easier to satisfy needs may lead to these unintended consequences. In the extreme, why should people learn to read or do arithmetic if computers can do it faster and better?

Haves and have nots—I don't trust "the system": What if better service leads to opportunities for a few and not for all? Wealth and power can concentrate, leaving out under-served populations and creating greater social friction and unrest. Investing the most in only helping the rich and powerful may lead to this unintended consequence over time—or expand poverty traps. In the extreme, why would anyone want a ruling class that exploits or ignores the needs of the rest?

Other foreseeable and unintended consequences exist. They all boil down to not investing wisely.

Let's explore what could go right with service. A golden age of service in the AI era is possible:

Great expertise—I trust "our collective learnings": Data-driven, science-based models that are improved over time means history is working for us collectively. The open and reproducible models are developed in communities of practice that are increasingly transdisciplinary. The models developed find their way into people's minds (logics), organization's cultures (architectures), and AI systems. The expertise of all people working to solve problems is improving over time, because of better pooling of collective learnings to improve service interactions and change based on better data-driven, science-based diversity of models.

Great collaborators—I trust "our shared future is worthy": The competition for collaborators is never easy. Customers and employees as well as citizens and immigrants can be seen as a type of competition for collaborators. AI-systems are being used more and more for finding a date or spouse, finding a customer or employee, finding a place to live and work or go to school or retire, and more. Entrepreneurs and policymakers search for compelling visions of the future that will attract investors. And yet, people often disagree with their best collaborators a lot, because that is part of a process of listening and improving each other's thinking about shared models.

Both what could go wrong and what could go right depend on investment decisions. Some investments can weaken trust over time, while other investments strengthen trust. Investing is more than time, effort, and money. Investing results in the fission (splitting) and fusion (combining) of communities of practice, as people sort themselves with like-minded others.

Investing Wisely to Close the Gaps

If you get the future you invest in, learning to invest wisely is a fundamentally important competence to develop. Long before people were investing in AI advancements, people invested in achieving better service in other ways. For example, building service organizations that overcome individual human limits of learning rate, social network sizes, and life spans.

First, we must acknowledge that today's AI capabilities are over-hyped. For example, the reality of customer service chatbots provides a simple baseline for measuring the truly limited commonsense language interaction capabilities of AI today. We know AI can be used to provoke conflict in social media and drive revenue growth in socially questionable ways. Can the opposite of provoking conflict, fostering understanding (better models) for win-win collaborations, happen as well?

Second, individuals, businesses, and governments as well as schol-ars, educators, and practitioners need to upskill and understand the right investments to make. While we do not want to fall into the trap of techno-determinism and simply assume AI capabilities will reach human level any time soon, we do want to prepare—by asking informed questions. In general, people who use AI (better technologies) with better models of the world to provide a better service to others, will replace those who do not.

Third, with the right investments, service in the AI era can result in better interaction processes and better change processes for business and society. However, explaining how this should/can/may/will happen requires creating and embracing better models of the world (science), bet-ter models shaping daily interactions of people (logic), and better models for business and governments to adapt to changing needs of customers and citizens (architecture). The models in AI systems, like the models used by people, had better be aligned with ever-improving data-driven, science-based models of the world, including the models of business and government built to serve humanity today and for generations to come.

Fourth, finding the best ways to invest that help everyone, not just a few, is important. An index fund is sort of like betting on humanity, or at least all the businesses that provide service to customers. For example, when you get ready to retire, you will learn about the 4 percent rule. As the rule prescribes, to retire comfortably and live out the rest of your life, you take the amount of money you need to live comfortably each year, say $100,000 and divide it by 4 percent (or multiply by 25) to get $2,500,000. If you have $2,500,000 invested properly, then you can expect over the remaining 25 years of your life, that you will have enough to live comfortably. Experts suggest an index fund is better than trying to pick individual stocks or time the market.

Fifth, equity and inclusion must be addressed in the investments. The first of the UN Sustainable Development goals is to end poverty. One of the most direct ways to end poverty is eliminate poverty traps. Ensure that even as the poor buy food or pay rent, that 1 percent goes to an individual retirement fund invested in an index fund that they can see growing over time and know they will be able to access when they reach a predetermined retirement age. Over time, people see that what they have invested earns them more than what they can earn from the market value of their labor, unless they upskill to amplify the broader benefits of the outcomes of their labor.

Sixth, the *right* investment strategy concerns people's data. If data is the new oil, then people need help monetizing their data. Imagine a platform that gathers the right data to reshape the investments that actors are currently making toward more mutually beneficial outcomes. People's smartphones gather data. There has never been a better time for individuals, businesses, and governments to gather data on how they are currently investing and shift the investments wisely away from activities that decrease trust and toward activities that increase trust. Privacy protection is a priority for responsible actors. Platform businesses are building models of human behavioral patterns. This includes individual buying patterns and levels of engagement on types of social media content. If scholars, educators, and practitioners could find an ethical and responsible way to share and mine this data, the potential for discovery and reshaping investments is enormous. The role of government is important in matters of data.

Finally, the first investment to make is in yourself—and learning to use the AI-powered tools of today to get and give better service. *People (practitioners, educators, and scholars) who use AI to get and give better service will replace (be more successful than) those who do not.*

1. Practitioners + AI = an automation/augmentation upskilling trend: Reflective practitioners in business and government are upskilling to serve their customers and citizens better. AI helps automate the routine activities of practitioners, making them more productive and helping them comply with regulations; AI helps augment practitioners by identifying others with better processes and higher-quality practices, and then helps them transform and improve their own performance to higher quality levels; AI helps augment practitioners who are experimenting with new practices that can lead to sustainable innovation, continuous improvements, and viable ways to broaden offerings to under-served populations.

2. Educators + AI = a knowledge rebuilding upskilling trend: Educators are upskilling to serve learners better. Educators provide the service of helping each new generation of learners to understand and use the best available models of the world. Educators see their own profession changing as AI changes the nature of what it means to be a helpful expert providing not simply a knowledge-sharing experience to learners, but a knowledge-rebuilding, cocreation, and future applications experience to learners. *In a fast-changing world, educators also help learners to ask hard question, to accept or reject models and challenge their validity and utility.* Educators equip learners with critical reasoning skills needed to reject and slow the spread of misinformation.

3. Scholars + AI = a transdisciplinarity upskilling trend (harnessing all the horses): Scholars are upskilling to build better, more comprehensive, models of the world. *Real-world problems do not respect discipline boundaries.* Better models of the world require building common language, propositions, and general theories to

interconnect communities of practice across disciplines. T-shaped (with breadth as well as depth) scholars embrace transdisciplinarity. A shared model of the world as an evolving ecology of entities, interactions, and outcomes exists in physics, chemistry, biology, and the social sciences, including the nature of technology and ideas. Just as AI translates between natural languages (e.g., Chinese to English), AI will help scholars translate between disciplines (e.g., economics and systems engineering) to build better models of the world.

Recall that responsible actors include individuals, businesses, and nations. *Every actor that gets and gives service is in fact investing time, effort, and resources in three types of activities—known as run–transform–innovate.* For an individual person, (1) run corresponds to activities that are routine habits (daily, weekly, monthly, and annually); (2) transform corresponds to activities that involve social learning (copying best practices from others, aspiring to be more like a mentor or influencer, etc.); and (3) innovate corresponds to unique invented activities that others may want to copy. Most people are not mindfully aware of the amount of time they invest in each type of activity. While a little thought or keeping a journal can help you become aware of your time investment in these activities, this is the type of data that platform companies are using AI systems to mine and monetize. Before you can hope to make better investments, you need some level of understanding about the way you are currently investing your most precious resource—time.

It is up to you to decide how much effort to put into learning to invest more systematically in becoming a better future version of yourself. Learning to invest in upskilling to both give and get better service is the upward spiral we are encouraging. It begins with asking yourself questions about your unique situation. It just takes five minutes to start your own plan, such as an individual learning plan or a service innovation roadmap (SIR). In just five minutes of reflection, you can begin to make explicit your learning investments across these three types of activities—time for routine habits done daily, time for social learning from others, and time for creative reflection and responsible innovation.

The world of service in the AI era is dawning. We hope this little one-hour-to-read book has helped you to pause, reflect, and begin to prepare.

The end notes will help you go deeper and perhaps find the right questions to ask—questions unique to you situation and the service-for-service exchanges most meaningful in your life. Asking the right questions, based on using better models, is the key to investing wisely in X+AI service-for-service exchange.

Conclusion

AI is coming to improve your daily interactions with others, but it is not quite here yet. Any busy person who has ever *wrestled* with an online chatbot, repeatedly typed *agent* and been ignored, timed out, or directed to trivial content on the service provider's websites, clearly knows businesses still have a long way to go to realize the vision of service in the AI era.

What steps should be taken to realize the vision of improved service in the AI era? How should responsible actors invest to become better future versions of themselves as X+AI? How will X+AI (everything with an AI-powered digital twin) improve service productivity, quality, compliance, sustainable innovation, resilience, equity and inclusion, and more? And will X+AI accelerate interaction and change, simultaneously creating increasing volatility, uncertainty, complexity, and ambiguity?

There are no simple answers to these questions, but we venture a few theses and remarks as follows. We invite others to challenge and debate our point of view, especially those who are not yet part of the service research community of practice.

Concluding Theses

1. *Goods-dominant (G-D) science, logic, and architectures do not fit*
   Goods-dominant (G-D) logic is still reflected and dominant in science, logic, and enterprise architectures. This logic arose to explain supply and demand in an era of markets for owned, physical goods, but begins to unravel in an era of markets for accessed, information service. Increasing AI capabilities will accelerate the unraveling.

2. *Service, service-for-service exchange, and value cocreation are at the core of the answer*
   Service connects to everything and is defined as the application of resources (e.g., knowledge) for the benefit of another. Service in the AI era promises to change the nature of both capabilities and interactions, improving win-win outcomes, if we invest wisely—starting with

investment in ourselves. X+AI service-for-service exchange holds the promise of growing the *resources pie* for everyone, increasing access for all, including historically under-served populations, but it requires responsible actors to learn to invest (systematically) in becoming better future versions of themselves—every actor and everything (X) becoming X+AI, gaining an AI-powered digital twin model, gaining an as-a-service capability that never sleeps and never stops learning to build better models of itself, others, and the environment of service-for-service exchanges.

3. *Service science, service-dominant (S-D) logic, and Service Dominant Architecture (SDA) as prerequisites*

A central prerequisite for answering the questions about service in the AI era is to first understand service itself better. This book examines service from the three perspectives service science, S-D logic, and SDA:

Service science

Science exists within communities of practice working to improve useful models of the world. Brains also build models of the world. Building AI systems involves building models of the world too. Service science builds and organizes new knowledge and experience on the subject of service as win-win interactions and outcomes for all actors. The application of conceptual, qualitative and quantitative methods to build better models of responsible actors' processes (mechanisms) for interaction and change is key. As an emerging transdiscipline (harnessing all the horses), service science models service and its essential interrelationships and abstracts them as service systems (responsible actors) interconnected by value propositions, viewed as an evolving ecology. All disciplines, including the natural, social, practical (engineering, management, legal, etc.), and formal sciences and arts, are communities of practice that are on transdisciplinary trajectories of their own. Just as AI systems are improving translating between natural languages, AI system will improve in translating between disciplinary languages and their data-driven scientific findings.

Service-dominant (S-D) logic

Logics exist within the minds of people and become dominant when they improve people's capabilities for interactions and outcomes. S-D logic takes a broad view of the context and role of economic exchange in society to try to understand how value is cocreated through systems of exchange. This alternative logic has been called service-dominant (S-D) logic, because it maintains that this exchange is better understood in terms of service-for-service than in terms of goods-for-goods or goods-for-money (value-for-value). That is, it is about the process and outcome of actors (e.g., people and organizations) applying their resources, such as knowledge, for the benefit of others—that is, service provision—in exchange for others providing service for them.

Service Dominant Architecture (SDA)

Architectures exist within the culture of organizations and become dominant when they improve organizations' capabilities for adapting to change. SDA is an emerging architecture putting the findings, logics and processes of service science and S-D logic into practice. SDA empowers responsible actors to act in the era of X+AI and in the context of openness and connectivity in a meaningful way and to organize service as a transdisciplinary process of value cocreation. That is rearchitecting the operating architectures from goods based, reactive, and siloed to platform based, proactive, open, and AI-centric.

Concluding Remarks

The greatest danger in times of turbulence is not the turbulence: it is to act with yesterday's G-D logic.

To realize the vision of service in the AI era and to become better future versions of ourselves in a world of increasing capabilities, connectivity, complexity, and ambiguity, we need to invest in upskilling ourselves to understand service and service-for-service exchange.

It is about rearchitecting societies, educational systems, and organizations to realize the advantages that are possible from openly accessible, participatory platforms that prepare people for service-for-service exchange, value cocreation, and service innovations in the AI era.

Taken together, the message of the book is that busy and curious people should upskill and invest wisely in becoming better future versions of themselves, and that while *solving AI = human-level AI* is likely still decades away, we will get what we invest in as a society, as businesses, and as individuals. So, learn to invest wisely in the service you offer to others in the AI era.

End Notes

Prologue

A prologue is usually the back story of how the authors came to write a book. The prologue of this book did not mention the several dinners at conferences where the authors asked each other questions incessantly. *We disagreed on many things, but all agreed on the centrality of service to generate answers—even as we struggled to align our perspectives and find the right questions.* We also agreed that the artificial intelligence (AI) of today is in its early stages, and therefore *just another technology* with the potential to improve service. However, if human-like AI could be achieved, that would not simply be another technology—but something different.

We recalled situations, where if we could have only asked the right question, the situation would have been resolved better. For lack of the right question, situations can unfold in unnecessarily less optimal ways. This short book offers *a peak* into our struggles to ask the right questions, which will inform both theory and practice, as the era of AI begins to unfold and massively impact that nature of service and our lives. To get to the right questions, we must reconcile more disciplines, professions, and cultures, and we need to expand the *big tent* of the service research community to be even more inclusive. We need to try to build better models to understand the world in all its diversity, intertwined natural and social systems. We need to begin to ask the *right questions* and invest wisely to shape the outcome. This book is our attempt to invite others into our dinner conversations—starting with what we agreed on—*the centrality of service.*

We realize that our quest to ask the *right questions* may confuse readers looking for concise actionable answers. While the core book is very short, the large number of abstractions, few examples, and lack of figures will be a barrier to many—though the end notes contain references with abundant examples and diagrams, a general audience may have little motivation to invest time and effort to *dig them out.*

The simple action that we would like the average reader to take after skimming the core book is simply to pause and reflect—"Are you investing wisely in upskilling to give and get better service, and to use today's AI, while preparing for tomorrow's AI?"

The complex action that we would like some readers to take after delving more deeply into the end notes is to help us define the right questions. Working on the right questions will impact both theory (better models) and practice (more win-win outcomes). What are the right questions to ask regarding service in the AI era? How do the questions shape wiser investing to harness all disciplines to improve interactions and change for all stakeholders while avoiding unintended consequences? How should individuals, businesses, and governments be investing to improve service in the AI era—not just the AI tools of today, but the more human-like AI that may be coming—our *digital twins*? Our bias is to start with a basic understanding of service science, service-dominant (S-D) logic, and Service Dominant Architecture (SDA) because of the centrality of service.

The Centrality of Service

Vargo and Lusch (2008) argue for the centrality of the concept of *service* for "academic and applied marketing and public policy" professionals, that it is a "proper, accurate, and enlightening term," and an appropriate "organizing concept for extending, elaborating, and synthesizing these logics."

Without using the word *service* or the words *value cocreation*, Wright (2001) describes both biological and cultural evolution from the perspective of entities interacting to produce positive-sum outcomes. Biological evolution can be viewed as an unconscious process, and cultural evolution as an increasingly conscious process informed by enlightened self-interest.

Pierre Teilliard de Chardin (1959) relates increased consciousness of entities and their positive-sum outcomes—again without using the word *service*. Huxley's foreword notes that "Pierre Teilliard starts from the position that mankind in its entirety is a phenomenon to be described and analyzed like any other phenomenon; it and all its manifestations, including human history and human values, are proper subjects of scientific study."

Also without using the word *service*, but clearly looking for commonalities and differences between biological evolution and cultural evolution, both Simon (1996) and Deacon (2011) see increasing hierarchical complexity in the unfolding stories of both the natural world and human history. Over time, simpler entities interacting can lead to larger entities interacting, favoring certain types of interaction processes over others. Service is a type of interaction process that forms an autocatalytic set, meaning it creates an increasing quantity and diversity of processes like itself. Service begets service, auto-catalytically. Autocatalytic sets, including the evolving ecology of service system entities, form a complex system of systems, which can exhibit emergence (Vargo, Peters, Kjellberg, Koskela-Houtari, Nenonen, Polese, Sarno, and Vaughan 2022).

Burke's (2010) knowledge web (see also k-web.org) provides an interesting visualization of connections among concepts. Burke invented and patented an intriguing method to look at how people and knowledge are connected throughout human history (U.S. Patent 7,292,243). The technique underlies his award-winning public television series and books. The connections he finds both entertain and inform, as seeming unrelated concepts, like bubble gum and atomic energy, are connected in a few short steps of human history.

Hopkins (2004) provides a history of the *Kevin Bacon Game* in the context of teaching graph theory (the mathematics of connections).

Arthur (2009) and Hawley (1986) view the human-made world as an evolving ecology. Human ecology is a highly interdisciplinary research area.

Human cultural evolution involves many capabilities (e.g., symbolic knowledge; see Somel et al. 2013, and Reckwitz 2002), technologies (e.g., spoken and written language), and organizational forms (e.g., businesses and governments), and specific social practices (e.g., cooperation; see Hare and Wood 2021, and Somel, Liu, and Khaitovich 2013) and traits (e.g., friendliness; see Bregman 2021, and Hare 2017). Thus, human evolution connects directly to service, as both depend on using knowledge for mutual benefits, on sharing and transmitting cultural knowledge by progressing collective norms and social order, and on applying knowledge and resources for creating new capabilities.

The Phenomenon of Service

Ricketts (2007) describes the pervasiveness of service in daily life.

The nature of service in society and the way it connects professions and responsible actors is captured well by John Ruskin (1860; 38–39):

> *Five great intellectual professions, relating to daily necessities of life, have hitherto existed—three exist necessarily, in every civilized nation:*
>> *The Soldier's profession is to defend it.*
>> *The Pastor's, to teach it.*
>> *The Physician's, to keep it in health.*
>> *The Lawyer's, to enforce justice in it.*
>> *The Merchant's, to provide for it.*
>> *And the duty of all these men is, on due occasion, to die for it.*
>> *"On due occasion," namely:—*
>> *The Soldier, rather than leave his post in battle.*
>> *The Physician, rather than leave his post in plague.*
>> *The Pastor, rather than teach Falsehood.*
>> *The Lawyer, rather than countenance Injustice.*
>> *The Merchant—What is his "due occasion" of death?*
>
> *It is the main question for the merchant, as for all of us. For, truly, the man who does not know when to die, does not know how to live.*
>
> *Observe, the merchant's function (or manufacturer's, for in the broad sense in which it is here used the word must be understood to include both) is to provide for the nation ... and it becomes his duty, not only to be always considering how to produce what he sells in the purest and cheapest forms, but how to make the various employments involved in the production, or transference of it, most beneficial to the men employed.*

Responsible actors invest to become better future versions of themselves. This can be thought of as the application of knowledge for the benefit of one's future self, as well as the benefit of others—change that leads to better interactions. Because responsible actors are conscious people or entities with legal rights (e.g., businesses, nations) with rights and responsibilities, responsible actors are complex systems. Complex systems can exhibit emergence (Vargo et al. 2022).

The Coming AI Era

The coming AI era refers to human-level AI (also known as artificial general intelligence (AGI)) and digital twins of people. We are not there yet. Progress in AI is hard to predict. Sometimes human-like AI is called broad AI (Hochreiter 2022).

AI is constantly in the news, but the general public has low AI literacy (DeCario and Etzioni 2021). This book makes the point that while the AI of today, such as talking to devices like one's smartphone, is becoming commonplace, the coming AI era of *digital twins* and human-like AI needs to be shaped by wise investing to get the benefits and avoid the risks. Wise investing has its foundation based on the centrality of service in the human world—especially addressing the needs of under-served populations.

AI is in the news because of massive investments, doubled from last year. Lynch (2022) describes the state of AI in nine charts, and the fourth chart is on investment, stating "4. Private investment booms: In 2021, global private investment in AI totaled around $93.5 billion, which is more than double the total private investment in 2020. That marks the greatest year-over-year increase since 2014 (when investment from 2013 to 2014 more than doubled)."

AI is poised for a breakthrough in human-like AI, some believe this decade, others in a few decades, some say never (see Progress in AI). Dickson (2022) interviews AI-leader Yann LeCun and writes:

> We learn most of these things without being explicitly instructed, purely by observation and acting in the world. We develop a "world model" during the first few months of our lives and learn about gravity, dimensions, physical properties, causality, and more. This model helps us develop common sense and make reliable predictions of what will happen in the world around us. We then use these basic building blocks to accumulate more complex knowledge. Current AI systems are missing this common-sense knowledge, which is why they are data hungry, [requiring] labeled examples, and are very rigid and [sensitive] to out-of-distribution data. The question LeCun is exploring is, how do we get machines to learn world models mostly by observation

and accumulate the enormous knowledge that babies accumulate just by observation? (p. 1)

Digital twins of planet earth (for predicting weather more accurately and faster than physics-based models) and medical digital twins of people are under-development. State-of-the-art digital twins are highlighted in NVIDIA CEO Jensen Huang's 2022 keynote (Huang 2022). Digital twins are computational models that allows for simulation and projecting possible futures.

Three Perspectives

We are writing for a general audience of "busy and curious people like us," who are engaged in a type of professional learning called reflective practice (Schon 1984).

The three perspectives of science, logic, and architecture relate to the perspectives of scholar, educator, and practitioner. Scholars help us build better models of the world, educators help make sure the next generation understands and can use those models, and practitioners put the models into practice, either commercially as offerings in businesses or societally as offerings in government. All phenomena have (1) discovery date—for example, data to knowledge, typically done by scholars and researchers, (2) first textbook date—for example, knowledge to curriculum, done typically by educators, and (3) first offering date—for example, applications, done typically by practitioners (Spohrer, Giuiusa, Demirkan, and Ing 2013).

Colleagues, Community, and Context

In the words of Roland Rust, one of the pioneers of service research, "The service research field is a 'big tent' field." Rust (2004) hinted at the disciplinary, cross-disciplinary, interdisciplinary, multidisciplinary, and transdisciplinary opportunities, noting that service research is "inherently interdisciplinary." Fisk and Grove (2010) provide an excellent, concise history of the service research field, as well as outlining future directions (see Saviano, Polese, Caputo, and Walletzky 2016, for related references for *big tent* service research).

Introduction

Interactions and Change

Butler, Hall, Hanna, Mendonca, Auguste, Manyika, and Sahay (1997) is a classic business paper about *interactions*.

Accelerating positive change in the world is a common theme of a number of authors. Auerswald (2012, 2017) paints an optimistic picture of the power of software and entrepreneurs to accelerate positive change in the world. Ridley (2011) is an excellent book for those optimistic about the ability to improve the human condition via technological and institutional change. Nordfors and Cerf (2016) and Cerf and Nordfors (2018) suggest a change in mindset could unleash incredibly positive changes in the world. Gada (2021) suggests that accelerating positive change is largely a matter of seizing the technological opportunity as it unfolds.

The flip side of people's good, value-cocreating interactions and changes are the bad, waste-cocreating interactions and changes. Reese and Hoffman (2021) argue that because of global poverty—requiring most of the human population to simply fight to subsist—most interactions are in fact wasteful, that is, that do not help individuals to achieve their full potential.

The challenge of avoiding unintended consequences is becoming an important topic in the service research community. Blocker et al. (2022) note:

> Service Practice and Policy for Unintended Consequences in Service: Throughout the history of modern management, change-makers could largely sidestep accountability for unintended consequences using the claim of bounded rationality, that is, "we don't know what we don't know" because problems are too complex to manage (Corus, Saatcioglu, Kaufman-Scarborough, Blocker, Upadhyaya, Appau 2016). However, the growth of data, artificial intelligence, and the ability to test scenarios increasingly weaken this defense. For transformative services, leaders seeking to promote well-being while mitigating potential harm are striving to identify, evaluate, and learn from unintended consequences. (Oliver, Lorenc, and Tinkler 2020)

This paper is one of several in a special issue of the *Journal of Service Research* on the topic of unintended consequences of transformative service.

Service innovation is coming to drive-thru's and changing the everyday, ordinary interaction of grabbing a morning coffee and biscuit, with investment from McDonalds and IBM (Fingas 2021).

Investments being made to change interactions are staggeringly large, with nearly $650 billion in venture funding globally in 2021 (Teare 2022). With private venture capital (VC) investments nearing $1Tn per year (not including investments from governments, large corporations, foundations, and other sources) and with global gross domestic product (GDP) approaching $100Tn dollars, VC investments in AI are approaching $20B per year. These well-intentioned investors and specialists create changes that may help some people some of the time and may have unintended consequences for others. For example, social media has changed daily interactions for many, but these are early days and even more powerful technologies are on the horizon. Investing in improvement is already happening at a large scale; it is how people, businesses, and governments compete for the future. The intentions of these *interaction changemakers* are to compete and lead in making things better for some. In a world that is increasingly technology-rich and knowledge-driven, the simple truth remains that when service is good, it is a good day. And when service is bad, it is a bad day. Change is often experienced as a new enhancement or unplanned disruption in a service offering from a business or government agency. People react differently to planned and unplanned change in daily interactions. Change is multi-faceted. Service offerings can be essential for quality of life (health care) or simply nice to have (entertainment). For both quantitative-efficiency (cost) and qualitative-experience (value) reasons, technology has become the channel of choice for a wider and wider range of service offering innovations.

The Organisation for Economic Co-operation and Development defines *online platform* as a digital service or technology-enabled service that enables "interactions between two or more distinct but interdependent sets of users (whether firms or individuals) who interact through the service via the Internet."

Some see interactions and change as fundamental service systems innovation. However, many times, service innovation is viewed narrowly as innovations done by providers interacting with their customers to improve customer experience (see, for example, Desjardins (2020) for the narrow view of service innovation, from a G-D logic perspective). Desjardins (2020) shows configuration (backstage), experience (front stage), and offering (system, performance). They pigeonhole *service innovation* into helping the customer avoid or recover from problems (*narrowest definition*) of customer contact service innovation. However, the ISSIP community promotes the broader notion of *service system innovation*, which is about all aspects of the system of systems. So, is *service system innovation* all types of innovation? Are there any innovations that are not service system innovation? Service is the application of resources (e.g., knowledge) for the benefit of another. Incremental, radical, and super-radical are ways of measuring service innovations.

AI Comes to Service

Mariani, Perez-Vega, and Wirtz (2021) provide a multidisciplinary and service perspective on AI in the literature.

Service Comes to AI

Mantas and Ramamurthy (2021) see AI-powered platforms as fueling winner-take-most industry dynamics (see also Turck 2016, on winner-take-all data network effects). Christian (2020) describes the challenging of aligning the power of AI/machine learning capabilities with human values, from the service research community (see also Barile, Piciocchi, Saviano, Bassano, Pietronudo, and Spohrer 2019, Barile, Bassano, Lettieri, Piciocchi, and Saviano 2020, Bassano, Barile, Saviano, Pietronudo, and Cosimato 2020).

Growing Connections That Strengthen Both

Wenger-Trayner and Wenger-Trayner (2015) are pioneers of the idea of communities of practice for shared knowing, learning, and improving performance. Engelbart (1962) was one of the pioneers of augmenting human intellect with technological tools, including computers. Steve

Jobs (2013) said, "When we invented the personal computer, we created a new kind of bicycle ... a new man-machine partnership ... a new generation of entrepreneurs" (Jobs 2013, 1).

1. Service in the AI Era

Quotes

Alfred North Whitehead (1861–1947) was a mathematician. His quote about how civilization advances by automating important operations is aligned with early notions of AI (Whitehead 1911/2012, 46). AI can be seen as automating mental operations, and the notion of service provision as a process of potentially many operations and steps that must be repeated at high quality and adapt to customer needs. Might such automation lead to a *thoughtless world*?

Roy Amara (1925–2007) was a futurist, who led the Institute for the Future in Silicon Valley, California, USA. The quote is documented in Ratcliffe (2017).

Herb Simon (1916–2001) was a Nobel Prize winner who learned it is hard to predict the future of technological progress. Simon (1965) demonstrated the early exuberance in computer automation of tasks, and dreams of AI capable of human-level business performance. The point of this quote is that predictions about AI have been very poor over the years, mostly overly optimistic. AI is very hard. In hindsight, we can see that Simon (1965) was overly optimistic about AI progress, a problem that has bedeviled the field since it started in 1956. It is interesting that he chose 20 years, which is about one generation. A typical person lives long enough to see multiple generations of people; grandparents to grandchildren is five generations for example. Also, in 20 years, as long as Moore's Law continues to hold, the number of instructions that a computer can perform at any price point increases by a factor of a million. A million times increase every 20 years seems like a lot, until one realizes that even at this fantastic rate of increase, it will not be until 2060 that one can perform a billion-billion instructions per second on a computer that costs a $1,000. That number of instructions is called an *exacycle*, and it is about the computational speed of a human brain. When Simon made his prediction in 1965, IBM mainframe computers (which cost about

$100K) were only able to perform about 1,000 instructions per second. Perhaps Simon envisioned computers with a billion instructions per second, which would have seemed huge in those days, perhaps enough to do work tasks that a business person could perform.

RLA Academy (2018) is the *true story* of AI that is told quite well in the entertaining online narrative by a fictional character, Zizu, a first AI, asking humans about its origins. Like many new disciplines, AI starts as bits and pieces scattered across many different individuals and organizations working under a variety of disciplinary names, including Automata Studies, Cybernetics, and Computer Engineering.

HAL 9000 is a fictional AI created by Arthur C. Clark (1917–2008), a science fiction author, who wrote the book *2001: A Space Odyssey*, which was later made into a film. Science fiction has shaped our understanding of AI–from HAL 9000 to Data in Star Trek: The Next Generation. In the story, HAL 9000 was activated and became a conscious entity on January 12, 1992. A conscious entity is a step toward a responsible entity, that is, a cognitive system entity is a step toward a service system entity.

Stuart Russell is a computer scientist known for his contributions to the field of AI.

Vijay Pande is a venture capitalist. Pande (2021) sees AI as the potential solution to increasing productivity in people-intensive areas of the economy, such as health care service, where costs continue to go up rapidly for routine and advanced treatments. Economists and the service research community are aware the challenge of increasing productivity for people-intensive service, also known as Baumol's cost disease, or simply, Baumol's disease, as articulated by economist William Baumol (1922–2017) (Baumol and Bowen 1966).

1. Foundations of AI: Automation and Augmentation

See Moor (2006) regarding the Dartmouth Workshop in 1956 and the origins of AI. For more on the two AI camps, automation and augmentation (augmented cognition), see Rouse and Spohrer (2018) as well as Spohrer (2020b). Engelbart (1962) is one of the early optimistic seminal papers on augmentation. Simon (1965) is one of the early optimistic seminal books on automation. The hype-cycles associated with AI have always tended to be too optimistic; for a recent example, see Wadhwa (2016). Too much hype eventually leads to an AI winter. Nevertheless, by Roy Amara's law the expectation is that while the short-run gains are overhyped, the long-run gains will be hard to imagine.

2. Service Robots and Platform Society

Service Robots

Service robot technology is receiving large investments, especially in countries with large and growing elderly populations like China, Japan, and the United States (see also social robot). Gaines (2022) describes Moxi, a service robot/social robot used in hospitals. There were many popular service robots offerings on the market circa 2020–2021, including in retail (Morgan 2020), telepresence (Nichols 2021), and home (Home Automations 2020). Wirtz (2020) describes the next service revolution and the differences between traditional self-service technologies (SSTs) and the more capable service robots being planned (see also Wirtz, Kunz, and Paluch 2021). Spohrer (2020c) provides some context on robots in retail (concerns of AI taking jobs), telepresence robots (possibility of AI creating more jobs with people as operators of multiple telepresence robots simultaneously), and robots in the home (reducing the need for jobs by lowering living costs for common household service expenses). Also, see De Keyser and Kunz (2022) for a literature survey related to service robots.

Even before the dawn of the service robot era, the challenges of industrializing and automating service operations have long been discussed in the literature. For example, Levitt (1972) and Karmarkar (2004) advise business executives to transform their service businesses with technological progress in mind. Spohrer and Maglio (2008) describe the emergence of service science to make technology-driven service innovation more systematic, introducing a Z-framework that describes the trajectory of a service from expert human to augmented-human to outsourced to automated. Spohrer and Banavar (2015) describe how the rise of AI will augment all workers in all professions eventually, and Spohrer (2017) describes the evolution of IBM's service business aimed at helping customers transform their businesses into a cognitive enterprise powered by increasing powerful AI capabilities.

Note that Baumol (2002) revised his cost disease analysis, showing that "research and development innovation" is the *queen of service*, and as long as there is innovation, productivity will rise eventually in all sectors. Fuchs (1968) details the challenge of productivity for education (when students as *customers* must do part of the work in order to learn) and for health care (when patients as *customers* must do part of the work to recover)—when the customer transformation depends only in part on provider expertise. With AI digital twins of the customer, even this may be accelerated in the AI era.

Platform Society

Van Dijck, Poell, and De Waal (2018) provide an analysis of the platform society and public values in a hyper-connected world. They see stronger government institutions stepping in if dominant private platforms become too exploitive of their users/customers or try to take all the profits and not share enough with the users and other partners (see also Spohrer 2020a).

How will AI-powered platforms help earners, who are busy people trying to earn a living? Torpey and Hogan (2016) provide data on both the growth in the number of gig workers and how much they earn on average over time. They also provide a nice summary of the pros and cons of gig work, why some people might prefer it as a lifestyle, and how others may become trapped or exploited in gig work. The International Labor Organization (2017) and the World Economic Forum (2017) suggest that there exist reskilling and upskilling pathways that would allow gig workers and workers to move jobs requiring higher skills and offering higher pay. Farrel and Grieg (2014) provide excellent insights on the difference between capital platforms and labor platforms, as two ways for gig workers to earn wealth on two types of platforms. They also show which gig workers can expect to earn over time. With more recent data, Sapjic (2019) likens gig workers to small business owners with perhaps a single employee, and then highlights the good opportunities and potential bad outcomes of gig working with a variety statistics.

How will AI powered platforms impact all sectors of the economy? Rodgers (2016) and Kenny and Zysman (2016) indicate that given workers' professional and routine service capabilities, there are clear opportunities to change the nature of service interactions to include AI-powered platforms.

Are AI-powered platforms the future of work? Autor, Mindell, and Reynolds (2020) provide numerous insights, including the role cities (urban centers) played in the past for upskilling for higher paid work, and the implications for how that is changing in an online platform, AI powered world of today. They offer numerous recommendations for how business and government can support individuals through these service interaction changes impacting work. They see responsible *private platforms* as the likely winners, and government intervention as ensuring that win-win outcome for future workers and platform owners (see also Van Dijck, Poell, and De Waal 2018). A growing movement under many names, including what Hunt, Simpson, and Yamada (2020) call *stakeholder capitalism*, what Mazzucato (2021) call the *mission economy*, what Moran (2018) call the *foundational economy*, and what was foreshadowed by the seminal work of Richard R. Nelson (1977), speaks to changing the fundamental focus and measurements of business and government to be better aligned for quality of life and individual well-being.

McKinney et al. (2020) provide an example within the context of breast cancer screening of how AI can reduce the workload of person and allow them to apply their expertise where it matters, improving both productivity and quality of outcomes.

Rainie, Funk, Anderson, and Tyson (2022) provide survey results of public views on AI and augmentation (human enhancement).

3. Questions

Practitioner question—predicting the future: Accurately predicting the future is impossible because of uncertainty and complexity in the present, as well as people's ability to *game the future* if they know what is coming. But that does not stop people from trying to predict the future—and in some areas such as weather prediction, progress has surely been made. Even in predicting future computer costs, Moore's Law has provided a good heuristic since the 1960s (see Rouse and Spohrer 2018). The generalization of Moore's Law is simply that the more investment an area gets, the more likely there is to be improvements in capabilities. See Baumol (2002) for a nice straightforward mathematical treatment of this general rule of investments generating improvements in areas where economically or socially important improvements are possible to attract more investments.

Educator question—automation and augmentation of knowledge areas: Sculley and Byrne (1987) describe the Knowledge Navigator, a futuristic vision of an augmented professor assisted by an AI agent with a bowtie. Historically, educators tend to be aligned primarily with a single academic area or discipline. Disciplines are a type of community of practice for knowing and learning in specific knowledge areas, and disciplines change over time (Wenger-Trayner and Wenger-Trayner 2015; Abbott 2001). In the AI era, it seems likely that more disciplines will evolve toward transdisciplinarity (Madni 2018; Mariotti 2021; see also Spohrer 2021b). The evolution of professions is related to the evolution of disciplines (Abbott 1988).

Scholar question—accelerated discovery. Some are working toward the goal of an AI winning a Nobel Prize (Kitano 2016). The challenge of accelerated discovery is well documented by Chesbrough (2020) in a model that shows it is possible to over-invest in one aspect of the innovation value chain and not reap timely business and societal benefits. He presents the systemic view of investment in three stages—generation, dissemination, and adoption—to realize the full value of innovations (see also Spohrer 2019). Friedman (2016) discusses the fact that what took a nation to accomplish decades ago (e.g., launch a satellite into orbit), a business can do now.

Consider some other directions and questions:

Digital Twins. In the AI era, better and better *digital twins* of all people, businesses, and nations will augment their capabilities, allowing computation to do more of what they can do, and soon they will be able to do even more with the help of more advanced technologies (to learn about the *digital twins* trend in service research, see West, Meierhofer, Stoll, and Schweiger 2020; see also West, Gaiardelli, Resta, and Kujawski 2018; Meierhofer and West 2019; Meierhofer, West, Rapaccini, and Barbieri 2020; West, Meierhofer, Stoll, and Schweiger 2020; West, Meierhofer, and Züst. 2021; West, Zou, Rodel, and Stoll 2020; West, Keiser, Stoll, and

Züst 2022). Taken to an extreme, *virtual immortality* would allow future generations to have a conversation with AI models of ancestors (Lenat 2016). How will having AI *digital twins* of everyone change notions of identity, reputation, and influence between entities? Will the very notion of people as *responsible entities learning* change over time as AI-empowered individuals, businesses, and even nations seek (1) to invest systematically to create improved future versions of themselves, (2) to play better and better win-win games with all stakeholders, and (3) to compete for collaborators, vast numbers of collaborators, to achieve bigger and bigger goals? AI may be the best tool yet for discovering the fundamental nature of humanity and the causes of human suffering throughout history. How do service robots and service platforms compare to what we know about SST, super-service, and the algorithmic revolution as the fourth great transformation of service (Meuter, Bitner, Ostrom, and Brown 2005; Campbell, Maglio, and Davis 2011; Zysman 2006; Bassano, Barile, Piciocchi, Saviano, and Spohrer 2021)?

Wealth for All—Ending Poverty: Digital twins speaks to the increasing technological capability of everyone, but what about ending poverty, creating wealth for all? Ending poverty is the first sustainable development goal outlined by the United Nations (2015). One suggestion for ending poverty is called *buy2invest* (Spohrer 2021c). Other suggested service innovations include that of Bill Ackman, as described by Ward (2020).

Brainstorming Exercises: A possible exercise for students is to propose bold service innovations and extrapolate other service innovations that would then be enabled. For example, consider digital twins and insurance: if a storm causes roof damage to an insured house, then the asset becomes aware of the damage and can initiate plans for and schedule the repair. Students can also generate lists of future service innovations and offerings, and then order them from (nearly) here today to far in the future. Students can also generate possible unintended consequences of different innovations. Students can be challenged to think beyond sustainability to resilience, and the ability to rapidly rebuild back from scratch or rebuild back after a disaster that reduced capabilities temporarily. Students can also be challenged about what they will do when the 100 or so apps on their smartphones *grow up* and become *digital workers*—what work would they delegate to 100 digital workers? What new higher order goals would they create? AI could lead to everyone having over 100 digital workers, dramatically increasing GDP per employee. What increased levels of responsibility and expectations will we have of each other in such a world? Challenge students to think of tools (resources) that are controlled just by a few businesses or nations versus tools that any individual can own, master the use of, and use in their daily lives. What does it mean to democratize a tool (resource)? What is the importance of universal education and standards? What are the similarities and differences between smart service system innovations (improve resource efficiency to achieve goals) and wise service system innovations (improve well-being for present and future generations), and what role can AI play in both types?

2. Science

Quotes

George E. P. Box (1919–2013) was a statistician. This quote is so famous, it has its own Wikipedia article called *All models are wrong*.

Marie Sklodowska Curie (1867–1934) was the first woman to win a Noble Prize. In fact, she won two Nobel Prizes. Her quote about "replacing fear with understanding" has appeared in numerous places, including Benarde (1973), which advocated an integrated systems view of people and planet.

Arthur C. Clarke (1917–2008) was a science fiction writer and futurist. His essays on the *hazards of prophecy* were republished in Clarke (1985). Clarke's three laws/adages are:

1. *When a distinguished but elderly scientist states that something is possible, he is almost certainly right. When he states that something is impossible, he is very probably wrong.*
2. *The only way of discovering the limits of the possible is to venture a little way past them into the impossible.*
3. *Any sufficiently advanced technology is indistinguishable from magic.*

There are many variants of the third law, including some intended to refer to advanced AI.

Isaac Asimov (1920–1992) was a science fiction writer and professor of biochemisty. Asimov and Schulman (1988) collected quotes about science and nature, and in the epigraph made the comment about science in service of humanity and wisdom. Asimov is also famous for his three laws of robotics:

> *First Law: A robot may not injure a human being or, through inaction, allow a human being to come to harm.*
> *Second Law: A robot must obey the orders given [to] it by human beings except where such orders would conflict with the First Law.*
> *Third Law: A robot must protect its own existence as long as such protection does not conflict with the First or Second Law.*

Thomas Kuhn (1922–1996) was a philosopher of science. Kuhn (1962/1986) is the seminal book about scientific paradigms and change. It is also landmark in explaining scientific progress as the professional activity of finding errors in theories, and when enough errors accumulate, this opens door for new paradigms and the proposal of new theories and so on, never finding ultimate truth—but gaining more useful knowledge about the world as the process continues. The Kuhn quote here is especially interesting because in the social sciences, new paradigms do in fact change the way the world operates! This is because people behave differently based on what they know and believe. Service as the application of knowledge for mutual benefit, which is a truly distinctive characteristic of people's interactions with each other, changes when we change our knowledge and beliefs about the world, each other, and ourselves. The community of practice of all scientists is, therefore, within the realm of the social scientists, even if the scientists are studying natural phenomena, where supposedly the laws of nature do not change.

Stephen Jay Kline (1922–1997) was a professor of engineering at Stanford, well known for his contributions to fluid dynamics and improving airplane and car efficiencies, and also for his work on multidisciplinary thinking. Kline (1995) is a must-read for anyone truly interested in developing deep knowledge of service science. As a mechanical engineer interested in systems and multidisciplinary thinking, he developed concepts for accelerating the socio-technical system design loop, which is related to intelligence augmentation. At Stanford, he created the science-technology-and-policy center and related programs to address in part the challenge of integrating across disciplines.

4. Foundations of the Sciences

Deutsch (2012) argues both for science as the best way to generate better explanations of the world, and for the importance of the scientific method for ensuring that a *good* scientific explanation comes along with a *solid* procedure for how best (most confidently) to test and potentially disprove that explanation. Explanations that cannot be disproven have little scientific value according to Deutsch. After reading the book, one is left with many questions, including: are there limits to science and the human capability to improve scientific explanations? Improving explanations is also a hot topic for trusted AI and the adoption of AI in business and society.

Regarding investments in science and R&D to improve service productivity, Baumol (2002) demonstrates mathematically that as long as science and technology progress has non-negative productivity, over time, the services sector can improve productivity, quality, and growth (knowledge-driven service growth). He also notes (in the way that economists of his era viewed services as intangible goods) that knowledge is an intangible good—and so R&D is part of the service sector. Baumol (2002) is also worth reading because in this article, he recants his famous *Baumol Disease* curse on the services sector. The article is also worth reading because of evidence presented that during the great depression, there was an increase in universities and R&D.

5. Service Science

Science, the result of social or cultural evolution, comprises both a community of practice and a set of technological tools and empirical processes for building better models and explanations of the world (Kuhn 1962/1986; Deutsch 2012). Both the science and AI communities of practice have processes for creating better models.

Service science is based on the idea of an evolving ecology of responsible entities interacting. Biological evolution provides a useful metaphor for thinking about social evolution and the fitness of entities' strategies in a social environment of other entities—also called complexity economics (Arthur 2021). Much of the literature of social and cultural evolution is relevant to service science. Biological evolution gave rise to neurons and brains, the interaction strategies of busy, brainy people are driving cultural evolution. And today, busy, brainy people are creating AI technologies.

An Evolving Ecology

According to Maglio, Vargo, Caswell, and Spohrer (2009), the noteworthy pattern of interactions between entities can be described by the interact–service–propose–agree–realize (ISPAR) model. In practice, all the service system entities that are interacting are, in fact, responsible entities, such as people, businesses, and governments (e.g., see also Spohrer 2021a). Service science is a subdiscipline of systems sciences/social sciences that studies an evolving ecology of responsible entities interacting, much as biology is a subdiscipline of systems sciences/natural sciences that studies an evolving ecology of DNA-based organisms interacting (Spohrer, Demirkan, and Krishna 2011; Spohrer 2016).

Kristan (2016) presents additional information about how neurons and brains came to be observed in the fossil record, including, for instance, in tribolites some 521 million years ago. It is remarkable that neurons are arguably only a billion years old, brains are only about 500 million years old, brains in flying social insects 200 million years old, and brains attached to opposable-thumbs in early-human-like primates only two million years old. Embodied brains are important for their ability to build models of the world. Brains store knowledge, and bodies put knowledge into action in living creatures with brains.

Seabright (2010) provides interesting details on the evolution of social entities that can trust, make and keep promises, and invent better and better value propositions. This *upward spiral* of social complexity is also mentioned by Wright (2001), who argues that the key to evolution—biological and social—lies in nonzero-sum interactions. Similarly, Friedman (2008) sees morals—that is, "a group's shared understanding of what's right and what's wrong"—as key to culture and cooperation.

Normann (2001) describes the challenges of social world of ideas. Searle (1997) introduces the idea of institutional facts to describe similar challenges. For example, dictators may define hunger as both fake news and unpatriotic. Lack of patriotism is a cause for imprisonment or death. Dictators understand institutional facts and use that understanding and their coercive power to benefit themselves and their families.

An Emerging Transdiscipline

Upskilling people to become more T-shaped, with both depth and breadth, is a priority across many industries (e.g., see Hill 2022, regarding engineers working in the defense industry).

Scholars advancing the scientific study of interactions and change in complex social systems sometimes refer to their efforts as transdisciplinary (Madni 2018; Mariotti 2021). Not using the term transdisciplinary, some scholars have identified T-shaped talent as industry's branding of the skills needed for a future of accelerating change (Gardner and Maietta 2020). The T-shaped professional and T-shaped skills metaphor expresses both depth (the bottom part of the T) as well as breadth (the top part of the *T*). *T* can also stand for *transdisciplinarity* from an academic perspective, as well as *teamwork* from an industry perspective. The literature on *T-shaped adaptive innovators* suggests that these people have communication breadth and problem-solving depth, as well as an ability to learn new areas more quickly, communicate more effectively with others, as well as other advantages over *I-shaped specialist* who know only one area deeply (Moghaddam, Demirkan, and Spohrer 2018).

Kline (1995) calls out cognitive science and AI as important overlapping disciplines that are promising candidates for creating an integrated overview of the sciences—and addressing the obligation of the elders. He also calls out the study of socio-technical systems as integrative across not only the sciences, but other disciplines like engineering and liberal arts.

In science fiction, there are many examples of AI systems seeking person-hood status, including in *Bicentennial Man* (film) and *Data* (Star Trek). In real life, only one potential candidate is known (Reynolds 2018). Sophia (robot) is the first robot to be granted citizenship (in Saudi Arabia), though it is important to read about the criticisms from the scientific community. The topics of animal rights as well as corporate personhood are related.

6. Questions

Trials are scientific business experiments. So in a way, business is a lot like science. Both perform experiments to learn and gain knowledge, about where to invest effort and resources, while staying within acceptable risk parameters. This often translates into "do more of what is efficient, effective, innovative and do less of what is inefficient, ineffective, not-future-ready." Both types of pursuits, business and science, are about learning and investing resources more wisely over time as new knowledge is gained, responding to the unexpected, asking new questions always, and formulating new aspirations (better future versions of self, including businesses, academic disciplines, and of course the individual practitioners who constitute the industry or discipline).

Practitioner question—trials (scientific business experiments) in practice to learn faster: Ledolter and Swersey (2007) consider business investments as a series of experiments.

With new knowledge comes new responsibilities. What if you worked for a social media company and discovered that making users angry at each other and fanning conflict increased revenue for the company? Would it be ethical to use this knowledge to increase revenue?

Educator question—transdisciplinarity in education: Real-world problems do not respect disciplinary boundaries. So not surprisingly, as educators prepare students to tackle real-world problems, the educators themselves must become T-shaped adaptive innovators. Leading educators are in fact pioneering transdisciplinary trajectories for their home disciplines (Madni 2018). As we try to learn to invest in building a better world, both economics and engineering are first movers in the trend (Mariotti 2021). Kline (1995) suggests the notion of systems representation, human-techno-extension factors, and a focus on the accelerating socio-technical system design loop can provide the necessary foundations for multidisciplinary thinking, which may help educators and their students to see the map of all disciplines and how they interconnect more clearly.

Scholar question—trust in science: As institutions become less transparent and less democratic, trust fails (Tapscott and Ticoll 2012; Sen 2000). The same is true of disciplines, which can be thought of both as communities of practice and also scientific institutions of a sort—setting goals, approving methods and overseeing compliance (Abbott 2001). When science is less open and reproducible, more doubters become influencers, gathering followers (see also Grjebrine 2020).

The positive role models in both science and religion seek to develop and encourage critical thinking skills in people, as well as a genuine humility about the many wonders and mysteries of the world. Lennox (2020) attempts to provide such a role model on the topic of AI; his Google Talk is also well worth considering as an example of someone trying to integrate science, religion, philosophy, and technological change into a whole for open-minded people who are curious about how to get the puzzle pieces to all connect. In a free society, people are entitled to their own opinions, but how do we evaluate the relative quality of the supporting ideas and the relative influence (and biases) of the opinion holder? What are the responsibilities of platform owners in making these determinations when they can amplify the opinions of influencers to more people than at any other time in human history?

Consider some other directions and questions:

Rapidly rebuilding from scratch: Science and technology co-evolve (Arthur 2009). Spohrer (2012) proposes an approach *to rapidly* rebuilding societal infrastructure as an engineering challenge—both as a way to educate the next generation about science and technology and to have teams explore for and possibly find shorter development paths that can be used if there is a need to rapidly rebuild from scratch after a natural or human-made disaster (Dartnell 2015). In a sense, this proposal is to *replay the tape of life* for cultural evolution and societal infrastructure many times to explore alternative pathways. Would it have been possible to invent photography a thousand years earlier? Gould (1990) first proposed replaying the tape of life as a thought experiment for biological evolution, sometimes called a wonderful life or contingency theory. Reproducibility is key to scientific method—formal sciences like mathematics are always and provably reproducible, but you can always look for shorter and more intuitive proofs. Natural sciences have the advantage that the laws of nature do not change (or perhaps they change very, very slowly; see Smolin 2014)). Social patterns may vary by culture and have the problem of the observer in the system, so *objectivity* is out the window (Barile et al. 2021). Machines can do formal and natural, and platform companies have AI experimenting on users in social systems. Describe, explain, predict, control has been the basics in science and engineering of things (also see Spohrer 2015, and Spohrer, Siddike, and Kohda 2017, for further explorations of empowering makers to rapidly rebuild from scratch). When it comes to technology, the service science community can learn a lot from the appropriate technology global initiative, and one of its founding fathers E. F. Schumacher (1973/2021).

Possible relationships between philosophy and science: The philosophy of science as well as philosophical theory can be confusing. These are related to logics or worldviews that most people have and often use unconsciously. Logics and dominant logics are introduced in the next section.

Comparing and contrasting biological and cultural evolution mechanisms: There is a good deal more that can and should be done on this topic (Hoffmann 2012).

What good are scientific discoveries? Scientific discoveries deepen our collective understanding of the world, inspire wonder in the minds of the curious, and benefit society and business where possible from the new knowledge as well. However, reproducibility and trust are increasing challenges in our complex world. A pressing and urgent question for scholars is how to ensure that one can verify the truth of new knowledge. For example, a prism helps you understand that light is made up many colors or frequencies. A prism works simply and locally and can help you trust your understanding of the world in an open and reproducible way. The negative consequences of a population that does not have a common understanding of science and the technologies and policies built on a scientific foundation is already beginning to be experienced in highly advanced nations today. Service science studies transformation of responsible entities seeking to cocreate value and co-elevate capabilities. Would it be better to work toward a science of change? Transformation? Innovation? Learning? Evolution? Or is it better to think of a science of the entities? Of people? Businesses? Nations? Organizations? Economics? Resources? Intelligence? Strategy? Actions? Decision making? Political science? Investment science? Or is it better to focus on what motives the entities to act and interact in various environments? Or to focus on what entities build and create? Design science? Engineering science? Public policy science? Capabilities and constraints science? Or to focus on the fact that the entities are complex system of systems? Systems science? Explanation science? Or to focus on the fact that the entities are guided by value? Value science? Ethical science? Rights and responsibilities science? Legal science? What part of the elephant do we grab onto as the most central and fundamental concept? Isn't civilization science, a version of history, which is typically part of the social sciences? Can't physics, chemistry, biology, and the rest be considered a subset of systems science? Or does that hide the human-centric-ness of what service science aims to study and improve? What about a well-being science— that is human-centered and could be stretched to include the well-being of the environment and planetary life-support systems? What are future sciences in the AI era? Will they become academic disciplines? How will they relate to each other?

Real-world problems do not respect academic disciplines. If science is to serve humankind and help you understand the world better, act more intelligently, act more wisely, and solve real-world problems, does one science dominant? Should physics dominate because it is so fundamental? Systems science, because it is so general? Service, because it is so human-centric? Service science developed the systems disciplines matrix to consider this dilemma of relating sciences and areas of study disciplines to business and societal systems (Spohrer and Maglio 2010). If science is viewed as a knowledge creation service, how will AI transform the sciences, and what is the future of science in the AI era? Will an AI ever win a Nobel Prize? Can scientific discovery be automated for all disciplines? Beyond physics, biology, chemistry, psychology, social sciences, computer science/AI, service science, what are the future sciences? Is there an end to science? What are the limits of science? How can science as a service in the AI era be improved to better serve humankind?

3. Logic

Quotes

Peter Drucker (1909–2005) was a management consultant and author. Within the community of practice of management consultants, he fundamentally changed the logic of the way people think about the purpose of a business as creating new customers. The quote is a paraphrase (Drucker 2006; Lawlor 2022).

Albert Einstein (1879–1955) was a theoretical physicist. Within the community of practice of physicists, he fundamentally changed the logic of the way people think about space, time, matter, and energy. The quote is a paraphrase (Amrine and Einstein 1946).

Anais Nin (1903–1977) was a feminist writer. Her writings explore the logics around gender interactions in different cultures, places, and stages of life. Sheffler (2015) is the source of this concise Nin quote that ties to the Kuhn quote in the previous section. For the purposes of this book, we claim that once you grasp S-D logic, you see the world differently—all the service-for-service exchanges become more evident. People and their ideas are the source of the inputs to processes of interacting, as well as the source of the perspectives on the outcomes of the processes of interacting.

Johan Arndt (1937–1986) was a marketing scholar and the quote is from (Arndt 1985), which won the prestigious Harold H. Maynard Award for its significant contribution to marketing theory.

7. Foundations of Logics and Dominant Logics

Scholars may clarify the nature of alternative logics, and then advance a particular logic to lay the groundwork for a general theory (see, for example, Akaka, Kosekela-Houtari, and Vargo (2021), who do just this in the context of S-D logic and a general theory of markets). Hunt (2002) provides a framework to move S-D logic, and its expanding community of practice, toward cocreating a general theory of markets, indigenous to the marketing discipline.

Connecting human logics (embedded in biology of human brains) to AI models (embedded in software and hardware of computers) is a research topic of great interest. Unconsciously or consciously, *logics* are at work whether people are thinking fast or slow (Kahneman 2013). Within a community, logics are a kind of common knowledge used to guide thinking about the world. Metaphorically, logics are like cognitive and cultural versions of microscopes, reading glasses, and telescopes—they are like a lens that allow people to see and think about the world differently, depending on the particular logic used. Watching a science fiction movie about an author's fictional world requires adopting a temporary or contextual logic. People have logics that guide thinking and interactions in the privacy of their homes as well as when they are in public places.

Within the community of practice of AI researchers, the notions of logics (both formal logics and informal logics, such as naïve physics, common knowledge, mental models) are well developed (Fagin, Halpern, Moses, and Vardi 2004; Gentner and Stevens 1983). For example, Fagin, Halpern, Moses, and Vardi (2004) prove formal mathematical statements about knowledge representation and reasoning among agents, including commonsense reasoning, when a group of agents can coordinate interactions based on reasoning with the knowledge they possess and knowledge they assume other agents likely possess. In human development, this is related to the notion of theory of mind. For many communities of practice (e.g., cognitive science, psychology, social sciences, including anthropology and economics), the notions of mental models embedded in neural networks and cultures are also prevalent (Berger and Luckman 1966). The very notion of a community of practice is in fact a group of people who focus on the pursuit of a particular shared goal or concern while learning together and interacting regularly—building common knowledge or a shared logic of the world for achieving a common goal or addressing a common concern (Wenger-Trayner and Wenger-Trayner 2015). Logics are also associated with the process of sensemaking in organizations, which contrasts with decision making (Weick 1995).

A logic is a type of point of view or perspective on the world that people in a community of practice (scholars/practitioners/educators) share/evolve/shift toward as they increasingly discover/name/adopt/apply/teach based on words/lexicon/concepts/language dealing with a subject matter. Dominant logics tend to be more widely held by many people or may sometimes be more comprehensive/inclusive/integrative than others, thus providing a richer foundation for development of thought and practice.

Within the community of practices of business and management schools, and management consultants and business thinkers, the notion of logics, mindsets, worldviews, cognitive maps, schema, and paradigms are also under development (see Kingman-Brundage, George, and Bowen 1995, and Prahalad and Bettis 1986, 2000).

The study of alternative logics used by people, both everyday logics that naturally arise and scholarly logics under development in particular disciplines, and the more formal AI models (*neural nets*) used in AI systems, is an area of research that may have implications for the future of science and academic disciplines, and hence for the future of education and practice. Just as it is important for collaboration between groups of people who have shared logics or who have different logics, it is also important in human–AI collaborations to understand human mental models and technological AI models, including their relationships, strengths and weaknesses, and ability to explain decisions and actions taken (Lebovitz, Levina, and Lifshitz-Assaf 2021; Lebovitz, Lifshitz-Assaf, and Levina 2022). Alternative human logics as well as goals for AI (automation goal versus augmentation goal) can also affect the nature of collaboration in complex business and societal systems (Barile, Piciocchi, Bassano, Spohrer, and Pietronudo 2018).

8. Service-Dominant Logic

Within the community of practice and the discipline of marketing, Vargo and Lusch (2004) proposed shifting from the goods-dominant (G-D) logic to S-D logic. Not surprisingly, the service research community was first to embrace this service logic.

Service-for-Service Exchange and Value

As S-D logic began to further evolve in the marketing and adjacent communities, some people began asking, "why 'service' and not 'services' or some other concept like 'process' or 'value' or others that can also transcend 'products' and ' goods' lexicon of marketing?" Vargo and Lusch (2008) argue that the G-D logic created a false dichotomy between economic activity based on physical goods and intangible goods (which are typically referred to as *services*), and that by conceiving of service-for-service exchange as the basis of all economic activity and by defining the

general category of *service* as the application of capabilities and competences on the part of one actor for the benefit of another, there would be
no dichotomy between tangible and intangible economic output.

Service Ecosystems and Knowledge-Driven Value Cocreation

The community embracing S-D logic continues to grow and expand into
different areas (Vargo and Lusch 2016). As mentioned, scholars may clarify the nature of alternative logics, and then advance a particular logic, to
lay the groundwork for a general theory (Akaka, Kosekela-Houtari, and
Vargo 2021). Per Hunt (2002), the move from logic to general theory
requires cocreation activities generating more formal propositions from
axioms, as well as empirical studies that support the propositions.

9. Questions

Educators continue to try to find better ways to teach S-D logic to
students. Seeing the world as the history of knowledge in service can
truly change the way you see the world. Most people take knowledge
and service for granted—they do not truly *see* it because they have not
internalized S-D logic (for relevant discussion, see Johnson, Lusch, and
Schmidtz 2019).

Scholars continue to work on making S-D logic more operational
so that it is easier for practitioners to adopt its perspective. For example, Töhönen, Heiskala, and Männistö (2011) argue that a service logic
embeds three core logics, a customer logic (focusing on customer needs
and actions), an employee logic (focusing on employee skills and actions),
and a technical logic (focusing on interactions, tools, and outcomes).

Additional questions to brainstorm: If AI systems are doing more of
the reasoning, what will their logics be? There is already concern that
datasets used to train AI systems include human bias, and therefore,
removing bias from AI systems is of increasing importance as systems
become deployed. Ultimately, will all AI systems have the same logic,
worldview, mindset to shape their reasoning or will there be a diversity—
perhaps based on vendor or cultural lines? Can changing paradigms with
AI systems happen much faster in AI systems, where updates can happen

in minutes, than in human systems, where learning is slow often requiring generational changes? What are the advantages and disadvantages of rapid paradigm changes?

4. Architecture

Quotes

Jeanne W. Ross is an organizational theorist. The relationship between architecture and organizations is important. The quote is from Ross, Weill, and Robertson (2006, 9). Enterprise architecture is an emerging transdisciplinary topic at the intersections of multiple disciplines, including organization theory and computer science (see entreprise achitecture (software) and service-oriented architecture).

Kurt Lewin (1980–1947) was a psychologist. The relationship between architecture and the better understanding of change is important. The quote, attributed to Lewin, is found in Tolman, Cherry, van Hezewijk, and Lubek (1996, 31). A good architecture makes it easy to change what needs to be changed most often, and possible to change what is rarely changed.

Norman Foster is an architect and designer. The relationship between architecture and time is important. Foster (2007) says the green agenda is about survival, not fashion, and yet it is cool—a celebratory lifestyle. Foster quotes Thomas Freedman that green is the new red, white, and blue. He quotes Buckminister Fuller that we are all citizens of planet earth, and that everything will be miniaturized. Sustainability connects buildings, transportation, and energy—and the behaviors of people in cities. The quote is a paraphrase from Foster (2007).

Victor Papanek (1923–1998) was a designer and educator. The relationship between architecture and design is important. The quote is from Papanek (2005), which was originally published in 1972. We also like another quote from the same book: "Design can and must become a way in which young people can participate in changing society" (Papenek 2005, xiii–xiv).

Elinor Ostrom (1933–2012) was an economist and winner of the 2009 Noble Prize in Economics for her work on commons and institutions.

The quote is from Ostrom's (2009, 422) Noble Prize lecture and acceptance speech. Describing institutions, Ng (2018, xvii) wrote:

> Institutions are social norms and rules (Ostrom 2005). They generate recurring behaviors that also reinforce the norm. Eating with chopsticks, driving on one side of the road—these are rules that have been institutionalized. Driving can be complex, but if you understand and believe that the car on the other side of the road will not come over to your side of the road, you won't panic when you see a car coming toward you. Instead, you are relaxed because your actions are embedded in muscle memory and everyone generally follows the rules, making driving reasonably simple (most of the time).

Christopher Alexander (1936–2022) is an architect and design theorist. The relationship between architecture and pattern languages is important. The quote is from Alexander, Ishikawa, Silverstein, Jacobson, Fiksdahl-King, and Angel (1977). The longer quote included: "The empirical questions center on the problem—does it occur and is it felt in the way we describe it?—and the solution—does the arrangement we propose solve the problem? And the asterisks represent our degree of faith in these hypotheses. But of course, no matter what the asterisks say, the patterns are still hypotheses, all 253 of them—and are, therefore, all tentative, all free to evolve under the impact of new experience and observation." A pattern language describes a new attitude towards architecture and planning: "Each pattern describes a problem which occurs over and over again in our environment, and then describes the core of the solution to that problem, in such a way that you can use this solution a million times over, without ever doing it the same way twice" (Alexander et al. 1977, 10).

Mateo Kries is an art historian, museum curator, and author. The relationship between architecture and social design is important. The quote is from Kries and Kruger (2015, 72). Another relevant quote is:

> Combining fine arts and crafts under the primacy of architecture as a structured element of society, the Bauhaus strove for aesthetic synthesis, that is, its products were to meet the needs of a

wider public, thus achieving social synthesis. ... By making these demands on the designer's role and believing in the power of good design for the purpose of social transformation, the Bauhaus laid the foundation for what we would today describe as an extended design concept or social design. (Kries and Kruger 2015, 10)

Roman Jakobson (1896–1982) was a linguist and leader in the structuralism intellectual movement. His definition of structuralism is given in a German Encyclopedia of Philosophy edited by Sandkrueler (1999).

Anthony Giddens is a sociologist known for developing structuration theory of societal change. "The structural properties of a system are both the medium and the outcome of practices they recursively organize" (Giddens 1984, 25). The structuration theory can be related to the work of Alfred North Whitehead, who created process philosophy, and the notion that infrastructure improvements are what can advance civilizations.

Additional quotes, for consideration...

Applying Knowledge:

We take other men's knowledge and opinions upon trust; which is an idle and superficial learning. We must make them our own. We are just like a man who, needing fire, went to a neighbor's house to fetch it, and finding a very good one there, sat down to warm himself without remembering to carry any back home. What good does it do us to have our belly full of meat if it is not digested, if it is not transformed into us, if it does not nourish and support us?

—Michel de Montaigne

Structure: "Structure refers not only to rules implicated in the production and reproduction of social systems but also to resources" (Giddens 1984, 23).

These aspects indicate that the structure and dynamics as well as the effective value cocreation functioning at the levels of service networks and service ecosystems represent key areas of service research. Understanding the emergence mechanism and the evolutionary dynamics of nested (in Institutions, author's note) configurations of service systems may be the core interest of a possible general theory of service. (Vargo and Lusch 2018, 247)

Design: Design science research methodology (DSRM); a methodology that interprets design as an "act of creating an explicitly applicable solution to a problem" (Peffers, Tuunanen, Rothenberger, and Chatterjee 2008).

Design pattern: A design pattern systematically names, motivates, and explains a general design that addresses a recurring design problem in object-oriented systems. It describes the problem, the solution, when to apply the solution, and its consequences. It also gives implementation hints and examples. The solution is a general arrangement of objects and classes that solve the problem. The solution is customized and implemented to solve the problem in a particular context. (Gamma, Helm, Johnson, and Vlissides 1995, 360).

Design Pattern describe the problem, the solution, when to apply the solution, and its consequences. ... the solution is customized and implemented to solve the problem in a particular context (Gamma, Helm, Johnson, and Vlissides 1995, 360).

Organize: "To Organize is to create capabilities by intentionally imposing order and structure" (Glushko 2013). "Organizing as specifying the principles or rules that will be followed to arrange the resources (should I sort my shirts by color, sleeve type or season?)" (Glushko 2013). "In theoretical terms formal organization may be considered to make power liquid and for this reason make it possible for much power to be concentrated in few hands" (Blau 1974, 18). "Organizational Development as a concrete improvement of functional capabilities understood as improving the ability to adjust, integrate and apply the organization's resources" (Zolnowski and Warg 2018).

10. Foundations of Architectures and Dominant Architectures

For more details on enterprise architecture as described here, see Warg (2021).

Making Simple Changes Easy and Hard Changes Possible

Emergence of multinational enterprise architecture: Cortada (2019) provides a detailed history of IBM, not only one the first multinational corporations, but also one of the most enduring. Cortada also provides excellent details of the role of ICT in the rise of other multinational firms, and transformation of national and other firms through the use of ICT.

Standard enterprise models: APQC (2021) describes a leading organization with benchmarking datasets, and key performance indicators for many business functions (over two million datapoints). Component business model (CBM) is used for modeling business KPIs across multiple industries. The Open Group community developed The Open Group Architectural Framework (TOGAF) and The SOA Source Book for Service-Oriented Architecture (SOA) (The Open Group 2021).

Enterprise architecture concept: Enterprise architecture is not only the organizing logic for business processes and IT infrastructure, it provides a long-term view of a company's processes, systems, and technologies, enabling both immediate action and long-range planning (Ross, Weill, and Robertson 2006). Lankhorst (2017) presents enterprise architecture as the TOGAF standard, which is a dominant standard (taught by educators in information systems and systems engineering schools). Ross, Weill, and Robertson (2006) present enterprise architecture as strategy, essentially platforms/ecosystems, which is a dominant strategy (taught by educators in business schools).

How Architectures Become Dominant Architectures

Breakthroughs in productivity, whether the result of the industrial revolution or the capabilities of modern information technology, create an explosion of the available opportunity space and the vacuum is filled by economic actors, creating in a race to create ever more value (Normann 2001). The different architectures of competing economic actors will create a race to become the dominant architecture that has the patterns that best support the required changes.

Suarez (2004) provides a framework for thinking about the ways in which technologies compete for dominance.

11. *Service Dominant Architecture (SDA)*

Cortada (2019) describes the emergence of the multinational firm, as well as early adoption of automation, setting the stage for later accelerated digital transformation as proprietary, legacy systems became cumbersome *boat anchors* slowing change.

Emergence of Service-Oriented Architecture (SOA)

Erl (2004) describes the emergence and turn of the century state-of-the-art of SOA and the open enterprise software stack that began to replace closed, proprietary, legacy, slow-changing enterprise software stack—metaphorically, the change from cargo ships to speedboats.

Emergence of Digital Attacker Platform Architecture

Warg and Engel (2016) describe digital attackers with online platforms that disrupt more traditional businesses, predicting by 2030 that platforms will become the dominant business model, that high-performing digital players will be competent in agile, and that new corporate DNA with be customer-centric.

Emergence of Service Dominant Architecture (SDA)

For more details on SDA, see Warg (2021). SDA was derived from the knowledge base of the concepts of service science, S-D logic, and institutional economics, with the aim of putting the findings, logics, and processes into practice by facilitating actors in the process of value cocreation (Warg 2020). The architecture enables entities such as organizations to evolve roles and systems that by their implementation and mutual value creation become dynamic value cocreation configurations and by this service systems (Warg and Engel 2016; Warg, Weis, and Engel 2015). (For additional information on SDA, see Warg, Weiss, and Engel 2015; Warg, Weiss, Engel, and Zolnowski 2016; Warg and Engel 2016; Warg, Zolnowski, Frosch, and Weiss 2019;Weiss, Zolnowski, Warg, and Schuster 2018; and Zolnowski and Warg 2018).

SDA can be viewed from conceptual and applied perspectives (Warg 2020): Conceptually, it provides a structure or design pattern, and practically, the pattern is instantiated in a structure of five systems to facilitate the process and coordination of mutual value creation. The five systems of SDA are (see also Warg, Weiss, and Engel 2015; Warg, Weiss, Engel, and Zolnowski 2016):

1. *System of Operant Resources: The system of operant resources is the heart of SDA. It represents the workbench, where the various resources and capabilities are brought together and processed. For this, this system applies certain logics or processes. In line with S-D Logic, the focus is on intangible capabilities, previously defined as operant resources (like competence, knowledge, skills, software code), which are used and brought together to (co-) create value propositions. The emergence of value propositions is dependent on the achievable level of resource density. A high resource density positively impacts the possible combinations and thus the emergence and creation of innovative value propositions.*

2. *System of Interaction: The system facilitates value in use and value in context by enabling the application of capabilities bundled in value propositions. Interaction enables resource integration and service exchange between actors and by this new resources with value creating potential.*

3. *System of Participation: The concept of cocreation includes other (external) actors as co-producers of the value proposition. In this process the system of participation enables actor-to-actor orientation and the participation of other actors by coordinating actors and facilitating the process of resource integration.*

4. *System of Operational Data Stores (Data Lake): From an actor's (e.g., organization) point of view, data received and generated by interacting with other actors (e.g., customer) should be systematically recorded and evaluated in real time. In this way, data and knowledge about the preferences and the context of other actors like customers can be build up continuously.*

5. *System of Institutional Arrangements (service catalog): As rules, institutions enable the coordination of actors and the access to and*

use of resources. In conjunction with design pattern, institutions enable the coordinated creation of solution designs by connecting actors, and enabling the integration of resources.

The (design) patterns as architectural framework of SDA are summarized in the following figures:

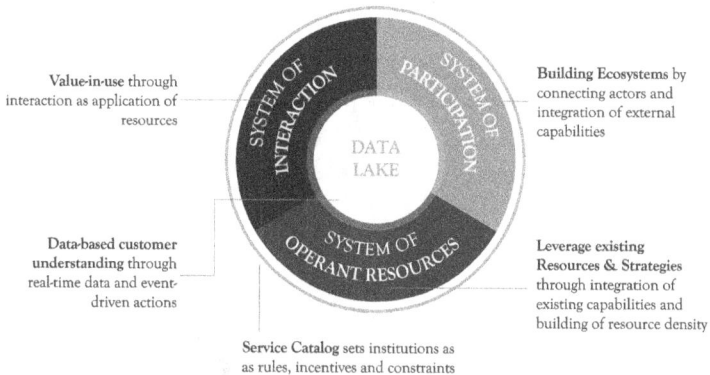

Value-in-use through interaction as application of resources

Building Ecosystems by connecting actors and integration of external capabilities

Data-based customer understanding through real-time data and event-driven actions

Leverage existing Resources & Strategies through integration of existing capabilities and building of resource density

Service Catalog sets institutions as as rules, incentives and constraints

SYSTEM OF INTERACTION / SYSTEM OF PARTICIPATION / SYSTEM OF OPERANT RESOURCES / DATA LAKE

Figure E.1 Design pattern of SDA

Source: IfSD.hamburg.

Detailed information on use cases and other technical implementation can be found at https://www.ifsd.hamburg/SERVICE-DOMINANT-ARCHITECTURE-SDA/.

Actor engagement: Value cocreation is difficult to observe empirically, whereas actor engagement is observable and thus more likely to be designable and manageable. Storbacka, Brodie, Bohmann, Maglio, and Nenonen (2016) explore actor engagement as a microfoundation for value cocreation.

Competing in the AI era: The following are essential requirements to be competitive in the AI era (based on Iansiti and Lakhani 2020): openness (platform organization); responsiveness; unlimited connectivity; agile; AI centric; powerful analytics; scalable; cloud based; real-time processing; rapid deployment of AI solutions; proactive; consistent; data architecture; composable architecture (packaged business capabilities);

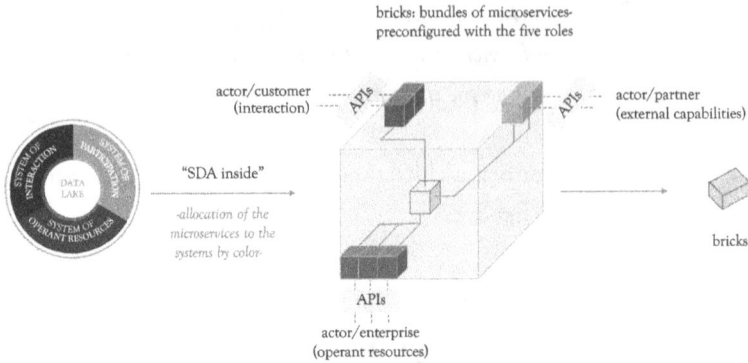

bricks: bundles of microservices-
preconfigured with the five roles

Figure E.2 Bricks and stacks as bundles of microservices—preconfigured with the five systems

Source: IfSD.hamburg.

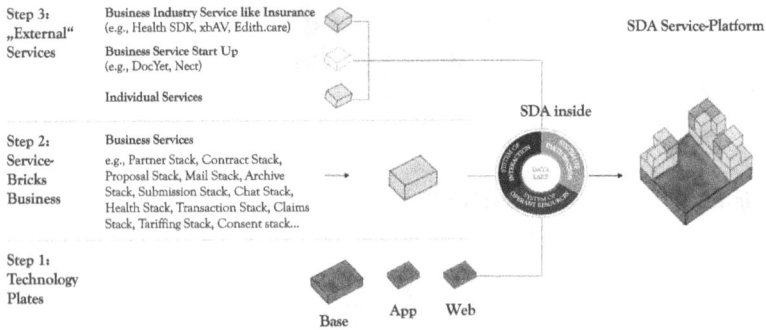

Figure E.3 Composable service platform

Source: IfSD.hamburg.

setting rules for the coordination of actors and resources (service catalog). Additional use cases are online at

www.ifsd.hamburg/SERVICE-IN-THE-AI-ERA/ with more explanations of the key concepts below.

Data architecture: Data architectures offer the opportunity to bridge the gap between powerful AI-based analytics and the highest standards of personal data protection. In this context, platform- and cloud-based data architectures are characterized by the following features, following the process of value cocreation: (1) the analysis of personal data takes place in the context of a specific value proposition, with the use of which customers explicitly consent to the use of their data; (2) personal data is located in standardized operational data stores (ODS) and do not leave the responsible actors (entity) environment, which are mostly cloud environments (technical instances); (3) AI comes to the data, and not vice versa; (4) for meta and transfer learning, the data will not be consolidated, rather the AI provider learns ODS by ODS (the models are exchanged not the data).

Digital transformation: Digital transformation is the profound and accelerating transformation of business activities, processes, competencies, and models to fully leverage the changes and opportunities brought by digital technologies and their impact across society in a strategic and prioritized way (Demirkan, Spohrer, and Welser 2016).

Lego construction: Based on a technological software production line (technical plate), generic and specific bricks are developed. In all bricks, the roles of SDA are reflected as preconfigured systems. The technical plate and the building blocks are coordinated through a service catalog as a set of institutions.

Platform organizations: The connection of platforms and existing organizations into platform organizations can be extremely helpful for incumbent companies by facilitating capabilities that compensate for their disadvantages in value orientation, speed, openness, and data-based customer understanding without losing their existing unique skills (Warg, Frosch, Weiss, and Zolnowski 2018; Warg, Zolnowski, Frosch, and Weiss 2019).

Service catalog: This sets rules and establishes institutional arrangements and thus enables the coordination of actors and the access (or constraints) to resources and capabilities. SDA service catalog specifies sets of authorized actions and facilitates governance and control (Ostrom 2005; Pichai 2018; Warg and Hans 2021).

Service design: Service design considers the patterns, processes, artifacts, and concrete solutions (value propositions, value in use) for customer experiences. Design is a creative act of finding applicable solutions for concrete tasks (Peffers, Tuunanen, Rothernberger, and Chatterjee 2008; Vink, Tronvoll, Edvardsson, Wetter-Edman, and Aguirre 2017).

Service ecosystems: Service ecosystems are "… relatively self-contained, self-adjusting systems of resource-integrating actors connected by shared institutional arrangements and mutual value creation through service exchange" (Vargo and Lusch 2018, 740).

Service innovation: Service innovation is embedded in actor-to-actor network (Lusch and Nambisan 2015). Service innovation involves rebundling resources to create new resources (Lusch and Nambisan 2015). Coming from a different direction, Arthur (2009) views innovation processes as evolutionary processes of combination and trial and error—technology creating itself.

Service platforms: Service platforms enhance efficiency and effectiveness by allowing more liquid and rapid of actor and other types of resource reconfigurations (Lusch and Nambisan 2015). As the number of connected actors and the density of resources increase, the need to apply an architecture becomes greater (Warg and Hans 2021; Warg 2020).

Value propositions: A value proposition is "[t]he co-developed understanding of potential value, or benefit, associated with a service provision—often articulated in the form of an implied or explicit promise and expectation" (Vargo and Lusch 2018, 740).

Workforce management: Over the past four decades, the service sector shaped advanced forms of interaction between human and technology actors with a wide range of actor combinations, such as human-to-human, human-to-technology, or technology-to-technology. The understanding of *workforce*, on the other hand, has remained largely unchanged in recent decades. Workforce, workforce planning, workforce management, workforce diversity, and so on focus almost exclusively on the human actor. The theoretical concepts of service science, S-D logic, social theory, meso- and microfoundations are suitable for describing the mechanisms of the wide range of actor combinations and the process of value co-creation. With the help of a new understanding of workforce that does not limit it to humans only but stands for all actor combinations that contribute to an organization (Frosch and Warg 2019), it is possible to explain and create the manifold actor combinations that contribute to organizational development (Frosch and Warg 2020; see also Frosch and Warg 2021).

12. Questions

The starting point for SDA is the question: What can we learn from service science and S-D logic to make the ongoing transformation of the enterprise go more smoothly? Are there ways of thinking about the enterprise architecture (both the organizational chart and the information technology capabilities) that facilitate ongoing transformation? In short, yes—service systems and A2A. Outside the enterprise is the ecosystem and institutions. Inside the enterprise are subservice systems. How is this different from traditional view of the enterprise as organization charts (departments) and IT charts (information systems)?

Additional questions:

1. What would a framework for describing all the types of service system architectures in the evolving ecology of service system entities throughout history be like? How would the fractal nature (self-similar across scales—individual person, business, city, state, nation, etc.) be represented, as all service system entities are responsible entities and resource integrators?

2. What are all the different types of service systems—beyond individual, business, nation, community of practice? What are the architectures of all these different types of service systems?

Service in the AI Era Revisited

The X+AI Vision: Your Digital Service Twin

The origins of the X+AI vision can be traced to Gelernter's (1991) visionary book, *Mirror Worlds*. Numerous others have imagined simulations of the world, nations, businesses, and people, but Gelernter's work still stands out for clarity of how it would happen and when it might happen, and for more fully exploring the implications than other attempts.

The modern practice of building real *mirror micro-worlds* is termed *digital twins*—and continues to accelerate, especially with respect to factories of the future and Industry 4.0, but also with respect to service systems (West, Meierhofer, Stoll, and Schweiger 2020; Longo, Nicoletti, and Padovano 2019).

Building digital twins of people is coming, as part of the coming AI era. For example, a digital twin of a person can be important in health care and medical procedures to simulate the likely progress of an illness or help predict the outcome of a drug or surgical intervention. Lawton (2022) describes some of the opportunities and challenges of digital twins in medicine: "Nvidia has been an innovative leader when it comes to new AI platforms for autonomous driving (Drive), robotic design (Isaac) and healthcare (Clara)... Digital twin capabilities are more challenging in medicine due to privacy safeguards, medical regulations and safety considerations. Although companies address these concerns in one-off implementations today, these are difficult to scale" (Lawton 2022, 1).

Digital twins are also a priority investment area to accelerate upskilling and personalized learning (Furini, Gaggi, Mirri, Montangero, Pelle, Poggi, and Prandi 2022).

What Are Some Gaps Between Reality and Vision?

Rouse and Spohrer (2018) provide an overview of the timeline for human-like AI and closing the gaps that exist to achieve human-like AI. The X+AI vision goes beyond human-like AI, to a personal AI that shares a cocreated hybrid identity with a person. Specifically, the types of service offerings that a person can provide are changed by the X+AI identity. Spohrer and Banavar (2015) provide an overview of cognition-as-a-service for all the occupations that make up a national economy, with examples from the U.S. Department of Labor's Occupational Information Network (O*NET) online database. McGowan and Shipley (2020) discuss going beyond T-shaped skills into the realm of X-shaped people, with the focus on an adaptive identity of a person, their AI, and their story.

Social learning. People are much better at social learning than other animals—it is a super-power of the human species (Bregman 2021). Developing AI capabilities for social learning is an area of high investment; however, the gap to human-level performance is still large (Pari, Shafiullah, Arunachalam, and Pinto 2021). The concept of social learning has potential connections to explore with the information variety model (IVM) of the viable systems approach (VSA) (Barile, Bassano,

Piciocchi, Saviano, and Spohrer 2021). To learn more, also see imitation, observational learning, and social learning theory.

Investing Wisely to Close the Gaps

To invest wisely in reaping the benefits of human-level AI and digital twins for service means (1) not being taken in by AI hype (while investing in "conflict resolution through deeper understanding" methods, not simple "more inflammatory conflict click-bait" that increases user engagement); (2) upskill on what investments to make; (3) embrace better models; (4) make investments that help everyone, not just a few; (5) including a focus on ending poverty to improve equity and inclusion, as well as addressing other United Nations Sustainable Development Goals; (6) ensuring personal data is used appropriately with proper institutional protections; and (7) upskilling to use the latest AI tools to evolve key professions associated with building better models (scholars), teaching models (educators), and applying models (reflective practitioners). For more on challenge (6), see Wladalsky-Berger (2022) on the widening gap between technological and institutional change. For potential solution to challenge (6), see Ng (2018, 2020, 2022).

See Spohrer (2021c) for more on investing wisely to end poverty, and see Fisk, Dean, Alkire, Joubert, Previte, Robertson, and Rosenbaum (2018) for more on investing to help under-served populations (see also Fisk, Fuessel, Laszlo, Struebi, Valera, and Weiss 2019; Fisk, Alkire, Anderson, Bowen, Gruber, Ostrom, and Patrício 2020; Fisk 2020; Fisk and Alkire 2021).

Smith and Shum (2018, 93) quote Hari Krishna Arya, "Teachers will not be replaced by AI, but teachers who use AI will replace those who don't." This is likely true for all occupations (Spohrer and Banavar 2015).

Lawson (2022) explores the topic of harnessing conflict for good. The social engineering required to harness conflict to increase the revenues of a social media giant is mathematically precise. Perhaps the problem is that responsible entities, media, and government are not properly harnessing conflict for good. If done properly, AI systems would help compile and analyze conflict of *bad day* service interactions for a new purpose. Logging and analyzing datasets are foundations for service in the AI era. Conflict datasets are fuel for debater technology and are replacing fear/anger with a more mathematically precise understanding, and perhaps making things better.

Becoming better future versions of ourselves. The gist of this book is that service in the AI era is about making people stronger, not weaker. If busy people who are curious about the world can harness the *bad days* to improve the processes of interaction and change to make more of the *good days*, then we are on the right path. To do this, we need better models of the world (science—scholars) in people's heads (logic—educators) and in our organizations (architecture—practitioners). However, these are not separate perspectives or roles; they are deeply intertwined in the transdisciplinarity of service, as a central concept. Ultimately, the self-service architecture of individual's time spent in three daily activities matter most—the logic they use to improve their routine habits, social learnings, and time for creative innovation. Both the individual (routine habits) and the collective (social learning) play a role, with empathy for under-served populations (creative innovation) also an important factor. The measure of a great society includes how they treat their weakest members (Collins 2005).

The key is to achieve mindful, meaningful well-being and resilience for future generations without becoming overly reliant or dependent on technology as a powerful, mind-altering, reality-altering, self-destructive drug. Filip (2021) provides a discussion of related issues, including an excellent summary and historical account of key perspectives on this topic from Licklider (*symbiosis*) to Harari (*dataism*). O'Gieblyn (2022) explores the nature of routine habits.

A short, clear book for busy people who are curious about the world: Did we succeed? Our intention was to write a short, clear book for busy, curious people from all walks of life to answer a question we get all the time, "What do you think about and work on?" The main part of the book is just the starting point for the longer journey suggested in the end notes—you can now go as deep as you wish down this rabbit hole.

Conclusion

Concluding Theses

For more on the future directions for S-D logic, see Vargo and Lusch (2017). For more on the origins of key terms in S-D logic, see Vargo and Morgan (2019).

For more on the future directions of service science, see Maglio, Kieliszewski, Spohrer, Lyon, Patrício, and Sawatani (2018). For more on the fundamentals of service systems, see Spohrer, Vargo, Caswell, and Maglio (2008), Spohrer and Maglio (2010), Spohrer (2011), Spohrer, Kwan, and Fisk (2014), Cardoso, Fromm, Nickel, Satzger, Studer, and Weinhardt (2015), as well as Wirtz and Lovelock (2021). For more on T-shaped innovators, see Demirkan and Spohrer (2015). For more on understanding human history, see Teilhard de Chardin (1959), Luhmann (1996), Hill, Barton, and Hurtado (2009), Tennie, Call, Tomasello (2009), van den Bos, van Dijk, Westenberg, Rombouts, Crone (2011), Whiten and Erdal (2012), Deresiewicz (2021), Graeber and Wengrow (2021), as well as Johnson (2022).

For more on the future directions of SDA, see Weiss, Warg, Zolnowski (2019), Frosch and Warg (2021) as well as Deetjen, Niedermann, and Warg (2021). For more on accelerating enterprise architecture change, see Braasch (2021) as well as Catlin, Deetjen, Lorenz, Nandan, and Sharma (2020).

For more on evolving approaches to research, see Leshem and Trafford (2007) and Blaxter, Hughes, and Tight (2010). For more on the challenges and approaches of explaining research simply for a broad audience, see Farnam Street Media (2021).

For more on human-compatible AI, see Spohrer and Siddike (2018) and Russell (2019). For more on the unintended consequences of change, see Spohrer (2022) and Blocker, Davis, and Anderson (2022).

Concluding Remarks

For additional perspectives on the future of AI in business and society, see Iansiti and Lakhani (2020) and Kissinger, Schmidt, and Huttenlocher (2021).

References

Abbott, A. 2001. *Chaos of Disciplines*. University of Chicago Press.

Abbott, A. 1988. *The System of Professions: An Essay on the Division of Expert Labor*. University of Chicago Press.

Alexander, C., S. Ishikawa, M. Silverstein, M. Jacobson, I. Fiksdahl-King, and S. Angel. 1977. *A Pattern Language: Towns, Buildings, Construction*. Oxford University. [online at wikipedia.org].

Akaka, M.A., K. Koskela-Houtari, and S.L. Vargo. 2021. *Formalizing Service-Dominant Logic as a General Theory of Markets: Taking Stock and Moving Forward*. Academy of Marketing Science Review.

Amrine, M., and A. Einstein. June 23, 1946. "'The Real Problem is in the Hearts of Men'; Professor Einstein Says a New Type of Thinking is Needed to Meet the Challenge of the Atomic Bomb." Einstein interview by Amrine. *New York Times*.

APQC. 2021. *American Productivity & Quality Center: Benchmarking Datasets*. [online at apqc.org].

Arndt, J. 1985. "On Making Marketing Science More Scientific: Role of Orientations, Paradigms, Metaphors, and Puzzle Solving." *Journal of Marketing* 49, no. 3, pp. 11–23. [online at www.jstor.org/stable/1251612]

Arthur, W.B. 2009. *The Nature of Technology: What It Is and How It Evolves*. Free Press.

Arthur, W.B. 2021. "Foundations of Complexity Economics." *Nature Reviews Physics* 3, pp. 136–145. [online at nature.com].

Asimov, I., and J.A. Shulman. 1988. *Isaac Asimov's Book of Science and Nature Quotations*. Weidenfield & Nicolson.

Auerswald, P. 2012. *The Coming Prosperity: How Entrepreneurs Are Transforming the Global Economy*. Oxford University Press.

Auerswald, P.E. 2017. *The Code Economy: A Forty-Thousand Year History*. Oxford University Press.

Autor, D., D. Mindell, and E. Reynolds. 2020. *The Work of the Future: Building Better Jobs in an Age of Intelligent Machines*. MIT Work of the Future Task Force. [online at workofthefuture.mit.edu].

Barile, S., P. Piciocchi, C. Bassano, J. Spohrer, and M.C. Pietronudo. 2018. "Re-Defining the Role of Artificial Intelligence (AI) in Wiser Service Systems." In *International Conference on Applied Human Factors and Ergonomics*, pp. 159–170. Springer.

Barile, S., P. Piciocchi, M. Saviano, C. Bassano, M.C. Pietronudo, and J.C. Spohrer. 2019. "Towards a New Logic of Value Co-Creation in the Digital

Age: Doing More and Agreeing Less." In Gummesson, Mele, and Polese eds., *Service-Dominant Logic, Network and Systems Theory and Service Science: Integrating Three Perspectives for a New Service Agenda*. Proceeding of the Naples Forum on Service. Online Book. ISBN: 978-88-31622-19-6. [online at naplesforumonservice].

Barile, S., C. Bassano, M. Lettieri, P. Piciocchi, and M. Saviano. 2020. "Intelligence Augmentation (IA) in Complex Decision Making: ANew View of the VSA Concept of Relevance." In *International Conference on Applied Human Factors and Ergonomics*, pp. 251–258. Springer.

Barile, S., C. Bassano, P. Piciocchi, M. Saviano, and J.C. Spohrer. September 27, 2021. "Empowering Value Co-Creation in the Digital Age." *Journal of Business & Industrial Marketing*, pp. 1–14.

Bassano, C., S. Barile, M. Saviano, M.C. Pietronudo, and S. Cosimato. 2020 "AI Technologies & Value Co-Creation in Luxury Context." In *Proceedings of the 53rd Hawaii International Conference on System Sciences (HICSS-53)*. [online at scholarspace.manoa.hawaii.edu].

Bassano, C., S. Barile, P. Piciocchi, M. Saviano, and J.C. Spohrer. 2021. "Exploring New Digital Age Challenges." In Leitner, Ganz, Satterfield, and Bassano eds., *Advances in The Human Side of Service Engineering, in International Conference on Applied Human Factors and Ergonomics*, pp. 57–66. Springer.

Baumol, W.J., and W.G. Bowen. 1966. *Performing Arts: The Economic Dilemma*. Cambridge, MA: MIT Press. [online at archivesofthecentury.org].

Baumol, W.J. 2002. "Services as Leaders and the Leader of the Services." In J. Gadrey, and F. Gallouj, *Productivity, Innovation and Knowledge in Services: New Economic & Socio-Economic Approaches*, pp. 147–163. Cheltenham, U.K.: Edward Elgar.

Benarde, M.A. 1973. *Our Precarious Habitat: An Integrated Approach to Understanding Man's Effect on His Environment*. W.W. Norton & Company.

Berger, P.L., and T. Luckman. 1966. "The Social Construction of Reality: A Treatise In the Sociology of Knowledge." *Doubleday*. (wikipedia).

Blaxter, L., C. Hughes, and M. Tight. 2010. *How To Research*. Fourth Edition. Open University Press.

Blau, P.M. 1974. *On the Nature of Organizations*. Wiley.

Blocker, C.P., B. Davis, and L. Anderson. 2022. "Unintended Consequences in Transformative Service Research: Helping Without Harming." *Journal of Service Research* 25, no. 1, pp. 3–8.

Braasch, T. 2021. *The Agile Insurer*. (www.strategyand.pwc.com/de/en/industries/financial-services/agile-insurer.html), strategy&, more information https://www.ifsd.hamburg/Leading-Use-Cases/

Bregman, R. 2021. "Humankind: A Hopeful History." Little, Brown, and Company. [summary on wikipedia.org], [book review on service-science.org].

Burke, J. 2010. *The Knowledge Web: From Electronic Agents to Stonehenge and Back—And Other Journeys Through Knowledge.* Simon and Schuster.

Butler, P.T., W. Hall, A.M. Hanna, L. Mendonca, B. Auguste, J. Manyika, and A. Sahay. 1997. "A Revolution in Interaction." *McKinsey Quarterly* 1, pp. 4–23. [online at mckinsey.com].

Campbell, C.S., P.P. Maglio, and M.M. Davis. 2011. "From Self-Service to Super-Service: A Resource Mapping Framework for Cocreating Value by Shifting the Boundary Between Provider and Customer." *Information systems and e-business management* 9, no. 2, pp. 173–191.

Cardoso, J., H. Fromm, S. Nickel, G. Satzger, R. Studer, and C. Weinhardt. 2015. "Fundamentals of Service Systems." Springer.

Catlin, T., U. Deetjen, J. Lorenz, J. Nandan, and S. Sharma. 2020. *Ecosystems and Platforms: How Insurers Can Turn Vision Into Reality.* McKinsey & Company. www.mckinsey.de/industries/financial-services/our-insights/ecosystems-and-platforms-how-insurers-can-turn-vision-into-reality

Cerf, V., and D. Nordfors. 2018. "The People Centered Economy: The New Ecosystem For Work." *Innovation for Jobs (I4J).* Independently Published.

Chesbrough, H. 2020. "Open Innovation Results: Going Beyond the Hype and Getting Down to Business." Oxford University Press.

Christian, B. 2020. "The Alignment Problem: Machine Learning and Human Values." W.W.Norton & Company.

Clarke, A.C. 1985. *Profiles of the Future.* Grand Central Pub.

Collins, J. 2005. *Good to Great and the Social Sectors: Why Business Thinking is Not the Answer.* Harper Collins. [online at whenthereshelpthereshope.com].

Cortada, J.W. 2019. *IBM: The Rise and Fall and Reinvention of a Global Icon (History of Computing).* MIT Press.

Corus C., B. Saatcioglu, C. Kaufman-Scarborough, C. P. Blocker, S. Upadhyaya, S. Appau. 2016. "Transforming Poverty-Related Policy with Intersectionality." *Journal of Public Policy & Marketing* 35, no. 2, pp. 211–222.

Dartnell, L. 2015. *The Knowledge: How to Rebuild Civilization in the Aftermath of a Cataclysm.* Penguin Books.

Deacon, T.W. 2011. *Incomplete Nature: How Mind Emerged From Matter.* W.W. Norton & Company.

DeCario, N., and O. Etzioni. 2021. *America Needs AI Literacy Now.* [online at pnw.ai].

Deetjen, U., F. Niedermann, and M. Warg. 2021. "How Insurers Can Act on the Opportunity of Digital Ecosystems." McKinsey & Company. www.mckinsey.com/industries/financial-services/our-insights/how-insurers-can-act-on-the-opportunity-of-digital-ecosystems

Deetjen, U. 2021. "Digital Ecosystems for Insurers: No One Size Fits All. McKinsey and Company. www.mckinsey.com/industries/financial-services/

our-insights/insurance-blog/digital-ecosystems-for-insurers-no-one-size-fits-all

DeKeyser, A., and W.H. Kunz. 2022. "Living and Working With Service Robots: A TCCM Analysis and Considerations for Future Research." *Journal of Service Management, forthcoming.*

Demirkan, H., and J. Spohrer. 2015. "T-Shaped Innovators: Identifying the Right Talent to Support Service Innovation." *Research-Technology Management* 58, no. 5, pp. 12–15.

Demirkan, H., J.C. Spohrer, and J.J. Welser. 2016. "Digital Innovation and Strategic Transformation." *IT Professional* 18, no. 6, pp. 14–18.

Deresiewicz, W. 2021. "Human History Gets a Rewrite: A Brilliant New Account Upends Bedrock Assumptions About 30,000 Years of Change." *The Atlantic.* [online at www.theatlantic.com].

Desjardins, J. 2020. *10 Types of Innovation: The Art of Discovering a Breakthrough Product.* Visual Capitalist.

Deutsch, D. 2012. *The Beginning of Infinity: Explanations That Transform the World.* Penguin.

Dickson, B. 2022. "Meta's Yann LeCun Strives for Human-Level AI." *The Machine—Making sense of AI.* Venture Beat.

Drucker, P.F. 2006. *Managing in Turbulent Times.* Harper Business.

Engelbart, D.C. 1962. "Augmenting Human Intellect: A Conceptual Framework." *SRI Summary Report AFOSR-3223.* [online at dougengelbart.org].

Erl, T. 2004. *Service-Oriented Architecture: A Field Guide to Integrating XML and Web Services.* Pearson.

Fagin, E., J.Y. Halpern, Y. Moses, and M. Vardi. 2004. *Reasoning About Knowledge.* MIT Press.

Farnam Street Media. 2021. *The Feynman Learning Technique.* [online at fs.blog].

Farrel, D., and F. Grieg. 2014. *Online Platform Economy.* JP Morgan Chase. [online at jpmorganchase.com].

Filip, F.G. 2021. "Automation and Computers and Their Contribution to Human Well-being and Resilience." *Studies in Informatics and Control* 30, no. 4, pp. 5–18. [online at sic.ici.ro].

Fingas, J. 2021. *McDonald's and IBM Could Bring AI-Powered Drive-Thrus to More Restaurants: Expect Fewer Humans Taking Your Orders.* [online at engadget.com]

Fisk, R.P., and S.J. Grove. 2010. "The Evolution and Future of Service." In Maglio, Kieliszewski, and Spohrer eds., *Handbook of Service Science,* pp. 643–663. Springer.

Fisk, R.P., A.M. Dean, L. Alkire, A. Joubert, J. Previte, N. Robertson, and M.S. Rosenbaum. 2018. "Design for Service Inclusion: Creating Inclusive Service Systems by 2050." *Journal of Service Management* 29, no. 5, pp. 834–858.

Fisk, R., A. Fuessel, C. Laszlo, P. Struebi, A. Valera, and C. Weiss. 2019. "Systemic Social Innovation: Co-Creating a Future Where Humans and All Life Thrive." *Humanistic Management Journal* 4, no. 2, pp. 191–214.

Fisk, R.P., L. Alkire, L. Anderson, D.E. Bowen, T. Gruber, A.L. Ostrom, and L. Patrício. 2020. "Elevating the Human eXperience (HX) Through Service Research Collaborations: Introducing ServCollab." *Journal of Service Management.*

Fisk, R.P. 2020. *How Serving Each Other Can Save Humanity.* TEDx Texas State University.

Fisk, R.P., and L. Alkire. 2021. "Service Ecosystem Health: A Transformative Approach to Elevating Service Science." *Service Science* 13, no. 4, pp. 194–204.

Foster, N. 2007. *My Green Agenda for Architecture.* [online at ted.com].

Friedman, D. 2008. *Morals and Markets: An Evolutionary Account of Economic Life.* Palgrave MacMillan.

Friedman, T.R. 2016. *Thank You for Being Late: An Optimist's Guide to Thriving in the Age of Accelerations.* Farrar, Straus and Giroux.

Frosch, M.W., and M. Warg. April 2019. "Whitepaper Workforce Design: A Resource-Based View." *Whitepaper—Institut for Service Design.* [online at www.ifsd.hamburg].

Frosch, M.W., and M. Warg. July 16–20, 2020. "A Conceptual Framework for Workforce Management: Impacts from Service Science and S-D Logic." In eds. J. Spohrer, and C. Leitner, *Advances in the Human Side of Service Engineering: Proceedings of the AHFE 2020 Virtual Conference on The Human Side of Service Engineering.* Springer.

Frosch, M.W., and M. Warg. 2021. *Workforce Design.* [online at www.ifsd.hamburg].

Frosch, M.W., and M. Warg. 2021. "Leading with Context—Impacts From IAD Framework, Service Science and Service-Dominant Logic." Paper presented at the 2021 Naples Forum on Service.

Frosch, M.W., M. Warg, and M. Lange. 2021. "HR-Management: Impacts From Service (Eco) Systems." Paper presented at the International Conference on Applied Human Factors and Ergonomics. International Conference on Applied Human Factors and Ergonomics; AHFE. 2021. *Advances in the Human Side of Service Engineering,* pp. 280–291.

Fuchs, V.R. 1968. *The Service Economy.* New York, NY: National Bureau of Economic Research. [online at nber.org].

Furini, M., O. Gaggi, S. Mirri, M. Montangero, E. Pelle, F. Poggi, and C. Prandi. April 2022. "Digital Twins and Artificial Intelligence as Pillars of Personalized Learning Models." *Communications of the ACM* 65, no. 4, pp. 98–104. See also video: https://vimeo.com/681877425

Gada, K. 2021) *ATOM: Its Time to Upgrade the Economy, 2nd Edition.* Business Expert Press. [online at atom.singularity2050.com].

Gaines, K. 2022. *Delivery Care Robots Are Being Used to Alleviate Nursing Staff.* [online at nurse.org].

Gamma, E., R. Helm, R. Johnson, and R. Vlissides. 1995. *Design Patterns: Elements of Reusable Object-Oriented Software.* Pearson.

Gardner, P., and H.N. Maietta. 2020. *Advancing Talent Development: Steps Toward a T-Model Infused Undergraduate Education.* Business Expert Press.

Gelernter, D. 1991. *Mirror Worlds: Or: The Day Software Puts the Universe in a Shoebox...How It Will Happen and What It Will Mean.* Oxford University Press.

Gentner, D., and A.L. Stevens. 1983 *Mental Models.* Lawrence Erlbaum Associates. (wikipedia).

Giddens, A. 1984. *The Constitution of Society: Outline of the Theory of Structuration.* University of California Press.

Glushko, R.J. 2013. "The Discipline of Organizing." *Bulletin of the American Society for Information Science and Technology* 40, no. 1, pp. 21–27. [online at onlinelibrary.wiley.com].

Gould, S.J. 1990. *Wonderful Life: The Burgess Shale and the Nature of History.* W.W. Norton & Company.

Graeber, D., and D. Wengrow. 2021. *The Dawn of Everything: A New History of Humanity.* Farrar, Straus and Giroux.

Grjebrine, L. 2020. *Why Doubt Is Essential to Science.* Scientific American. [online at scientificamerican.com].

Hare, B. 2017. "Survival of the Friendliest: Homo Sapiens Evolved Via Selection for Prosociality." *Annual Review of Psychology* 68, pp. 155–186. [online at evolutionaryanthropology.duke.edu].

Hare, B. and V. Wood. 2021. *Survival of the Friendliest: Understanding Our Origins and Rediscovering Our Common Humanity.* Random House. [online summary at wikipedia.org].

Hawley, A. 1986. *Human Ecology: A Theoretical Essay.* University of Chicago Press.

Hill, K., M. Barton, and A.M. Hurtado. 2009. "The Emergence of Human Uniqueness: Characters Underlying Behavioral Modernity." *Evolutionary Anthropology: Issues, News, and Reviews* 18, no. 5, pp. 187–200. [online at wiley.com].

Hill, S.C. 2022. *Demand Grows for Multi-Skilled, Flexible Engineers.* [online at nationaldefensemagazine.org].

Hochreiter, S. April 2022. "Toward a Broad AI." *Europe Region special section: Hot topics. Communications of the ACM* 65, no. 4, pp. 56–57.

Hoffmann, P.M. 2012. *Life's Ratchet: How Molecular Machines Extract Order From Chaos.* Basic Books.

Home Automations. 2020. *Top 10 Personal Robots 2020.* [online at home-automations.net].

Hopkins, B. 2004. "Kevin Bacon and Graph Theory." *Problems, Resources, and Issues in Mathematics Undergraduate Studies* 14, no. 1, pp. 5–11. [online at mathsci2.appstate.edu].

Huang, J. 2022. *GTC 2022 Keynote With NVIDIA CEO Jensen Huang.* [online at YouTube].

Hunt, S.D. 2002. *Foundations of Marketing Theory: Toward a General Theory of Marketing.* Routledge.

Hunt, V., B. Simpson, and Y. Yamada. 2020. "The Case for Stakeholder Capitalism." McKinsey Report. [online at mckinsey.com].

Iansiti, M., and K.R. Lakhani. 2020. *Competing in the Age of AI: Strategy and Leadership When Algorithms and Networks Run the World.* Harvard Business Press.

ILO. 2017. *Helping the Gig Economy Work Better for Gig Workers.* International Labor Organization. [online at www.ilo.org].

Jobs, S. 2013. *Bicycles of the Mind: Humans as Tool Builders.* [online www.youtube.com]. For more on the history of this quote S. Sinosky. 2019. *Bicycle for the Mind.* [online at medium.learningbyshipping.com].

Johnson, C., R. Lusch, and D. Schmidtz. 2019. *Commercial Society: A Primer on Ethics and Economics.* Rowman & Littlefield.

Johnson, S. 2022. "Change Of Seasons: Our Ancestors May Have Shifted Back and Forth Between Different Work Routines and Social Structures, Often in Tune With the Seasons. Would That Be a Better Way to Live?" Adjacent Possible newsletter. [online at stevenberlinjohnson.com].

Kahneman, D. 2013. *Thinking Fast and Slow.* Farrar, Straus and Giroux. (wikipedia).

Karmarkar, U. June 2004. "Will You Survive the Services Revolution?" *Harvard Business Review*, pp. 100–107.

Kenny, M., and J. Zysman. 2016. "The Rise of the Platform Economy." *Issues in Science and Technology* XXXII, no. 3. Spring. [online at issues.org].

Kingman-Brundage, J., W.R. George, and D.E. Bowen. 1995. ""Service Logic": Achieving Service System Integration." *International Journal of service industry management* 6, no. 4, pp. 20–39.

Kissinger, H.A., E. Schmidt, and D. Huttenlocher. 2021 *The Age of AI: And Our Human Future.* Little, Brown and Company.

Kitano, H. April 2016. "Artificial Intelligence to Win the Nobel Prize and Beyond: Creating the Engine for Scientific Discovery." *AI magazine* 37, no. 1, pp. 39–49. [online at aaai.org].

Kline, S.J. 1995. *Conceptual Foundations of Multidisciplinary Thinking.* Stanford University Press.

Kries, M., and J. Kugler. 2015. *The Bauhaus #Itsalldesign.* Vitra Design Museum.

Kristan, W.B. October 2016. "Early Evolution of Neurons." *Current Biology* 26, pp. 949–954.

Kuhn, T.S. 1962/1986. *The Structure of Scientific Revolutions, Second Edition.* University of Chicago.

Lankhorst, M. 2017. *Enterprise Architecture at Work: Modeling, Communications, and Analysis, Fourth Edition.* Springer.

Lawlor, B. 2022. *Did Drucker Say That?* Peter Drucker Institute website. [online at www.drucker.institute].

Lawson, A. 2022. *Building Trust Across the Political Divide: The Surprising Bridge of Conflict.* Comment Magazine. [online at comment.org].

Lawton, G. 2022. *NVIDIA Sets the Stage for Medical Digital Twin.* [online at venturebeat.com].

Lebovitz, S., N. Levina, and H. Lifshitz-Assaf. 2021. "Is AI Ground Truth Really 'True'? The Dangers of Training and Evaluating AI Tools Based on Experts' Know-What." *Management Information Systems Quarterly.* [online at researchgate.net].

Lebovitz, S., H. Lifshitz-Assaf, and N. Levina. 2022. *To Engage or Not to Engage With AI for Critical Judgments: How Professionals Deal With Opacity When Using AI for Medical Diagnosis.* Organization Science. [online at ssrn .com].

Ledolter, J., and A.J. Swersey. 2007. *Testing 1—2—3: Experimental Design With Applications in Marketing and Service Operations.* Stanford Business Books.

Lenat, D.B. 2016. "WWTS (What Would Turing Say?)." *AI Magazine* 37, no.1, pp. 97–101. [online at aaai.org].

Lennox, J.C. 2020. *2084: AI and the Future of Humanity.* Zondervan. [also see GoogleTalk discussion by the same title online at www.youtube.com].

Leshem, S., and V. Trafford. 2007. "Overlooking the Conceptual Framework." *Innovations in Education and Teaching International* 44, no. 1, pp. 93–105. [online at researchgate.net].

Levitt, T. September 1972. "Production-Line Approach to Service." *Harvard Business Review* 50, no. 5, pp. 41–52.

Longo, F., L. Nicoletti, and A. Padovano. 2019. "Ubiquitous Knowledge Empowers the Smart Factory: The Impacts of a Service-Oriented Digital Twin on Enterprises' Performance." *Annual Reviews in Control* 47, pp. 221–236.

Luhmann, N. 1996. *Social Systems.* Stanford University Press.

Lusch, R.F., and S. Nambisan. 2015. "Service Innovation: A Service-Dominant Logic Perspective." *MIS Quarterly* 39, no. 1, pp. 155–175. [online at researchgate.net].

Lynch, S. 2022. *The State of AI in 9 Charts.* HAI—Human-Centered Artificial Intelligence. Stanford University.

Madni, A. 2018. *Transdisciplinary Systems Engineering: Exploiting Convergence in a Hyper-Connected World.* Springer.

Maglio, P.P., S.L. Vargo, and B. Caswell, and J. Spohrer. 2009. "The Service System is the Basic Abstraction of Service Science." *Information Systems and e-Business Management* 7, no. 4, pp. 395–406. [online at researchgate.net].

Maglio, P.P., C.A. Kieliszewski, J.C. Spohrer, K. Lyon, L. Patrício, and Y. Sawatani. 2018. *Handbook of Service Science* Vol. 2. Springer.

Mantas, J., and S. Ramamurthy. 2021. *The Cognitive Enterprise: Reinventing Your Company With AI—Create Platforms to Unleash Digital Darwinism.* IBM Institute for Business Value. [online at ibm.com].

Mariani, M.M., R. Perez-Vega, and J. Wirtz. 2021. "AI in Marketing, Consumer Research and Psychology: A Systematic Literature Review and Research Agenda." *Journal of Psychology and Marketing*, pp. 1–22.

Mariotti, S. 2021. "Forging a New Alliance Between Economics and Engineering." *Journal of Industrial and Business Economics* 48, pp. 551–572.

Mazzucato, M. 2021. *Mission Economy: A Moonshot Guide to Changing Capitalism.* Harper.

McGowan, H.E., and C. Shipley. 2020. *The Adaptation Advantage: Let Go, Learn Fast, and Thrive in the Future of Work.* John Wiley & Sons.

McKinney, S.M., M. Sieniek, V. Godbole, J. Godwin, N. Antropova, H. Ashrafian, T. Back, M. Chesus, G.S. Corrado, A. Darzi, M. Etemadi, F. Garcia-Vicente, F.J. Gilbert, M. Halling-Brown, D. Hassabis, S. Jansen, A. Karthikesalingam, C.J. Kelly, D. King, J.R. Ledsam, D. Melnick, H. Mostofi, L. eng, J.J. Reicher, B. Romera-Paredes, R. Sidebottom, M. Suleyman, D. Tse, K.C. Young, J. De Fauw, and S. Shetty. 2020. "International Evaluation of an AI system for Breast Cancer Screening." *Nature* 577, no. 7788, pp. 89–94. [online at deepmind.com].

Meierhofer, J., and S. West. 2019. "Service Value Creation Using a Digital Twin." In *Naples Forum on Service, Service-Dominant Logic, Network & Systems Theory and Service Science: Integrating Three Perspectives for a New Service Agenda, Ischia*, pp. 4–7. [online at naplesforumonservice.com].

Meierhofer, J., S. West, M. Rapaccini, and C. Barbieri. 2020 "The Digital Twin as a Service Enabler: From the Service Ecosystem to the Simulation Model." In *International Conference on Exploring Services Science*, pp. 347–359. Springer. [online at flore.unifi.it].

Meuter, M.L., M.J. Bitner, A.L. Ostrom, and S.W. Brown. 2005. "Choosing Among Alternative Service Delivery Modes: An Investigation of Customer Trial of Self-Service Technologies." *Journal of Marketing* 69, no. 2, pp. 61–83.

Moghaddam, Y., H. Demirkan, and J. Spohrer. 2018. *T-Shaped Professionals: Adaptive Innovators.* Business Expert Press.

Moor, J. 2006. "The Dartmouth College Artificial Intelligence Conference: The Next Fifty Years." *AI Magazine* 27, pp. 87–91. [online at researchgate.net].

Moran, M. 2018. *The Foundational Economy: The Infrastructure of Everyday Life.* Manchester University Press.

Morgan, B. 2020. *The 3 Best In-Store Robots And Why They Work.* [online at forbes.com].

Nelson, R.N. 1977. *The Moon and the Ghetto: An Essay on Public Policy Analysis.* WW Norton & Company.

Ng, I.C.L. 2018. Foreword by I. Ng. In *Handbook of Service Science* (Vol. 2), Maglio, Kieliszewski, Spohrer, Lyons, Patricio, and Sawatani eds. Springer.

Ng, I.C.L. 2018. "The Market for Person-Controlled Personal Data With the Hub-of-all-Things (HAT)." Working Paper. Coventry: Warwick Manufacturing Group. WMG Service Systems Research Group Working Paper Series (01/18). (Unpublished).

Ng, I.C.L. 2020. *The Data Economy 2.0.* [online at medium.com].

Ng, I.C.L. 2022. *The Case for a Global Cooperation on Identity.* [online at medium .com].

Nichols, G. 2021. "Best Telepresence Robot 2021: The Best Telepresence Hardware to Go Beyond Video Conferencing and Make Remote Work Truly Collaborative." [online at zdnet.com]

Nordfors, D., and V. Cerf. 2016 "Disrupting Unemployment: Reflections on a Sustainable, Middle Class Economic Recovery." *Innovation for Jobs (I4J),* Independently Published.

Normann, R. 2001. *Reframing Business: When the Map Changes the Landscape.* John Wiley & Sons.

O'Gieblyn, M. 2022. *Routine Maintenance: Embracing Habit in an Automated World.* Harper's Magazine. [oneline at harpers.org].

OECD. 2019. "What is an "online platform"?" In *An Introduction to Online Platforms and Their Role in the Digital Transformation.* OECD Publishing.

Oliver, K., T. Lorenc, J. Tinkler. 2020. "Evaluating Unintended Consequences: New Insights into Solving Practical, Ethical and Political Challenges of Evaluation." *Evaluation* 26, no. 1, pp. 61–75.

Ostrom, E. 2005. *Understanding Institutional Diversity.* Princeton University. [online at wef.tw]

Ostrom, E. December 08, 2009. "Beyond Markets and States: Polycentric Governance of Complex Economic Systems." Noble Prize lecture. [online at nobleprize.org].

Pande, V. 2021. *Solving Baumol's Cost Disease, in Healthcare.* [online at a16z .com].

Papanek, V. 2005. *Design for the Real World: Human Ecology and Social Change.* Academy Chicago.

Pari, J., N.M. Shafiullah, S.P. Arunachalam, and L. Pinto. 2021. *The Surprising Effectiveness of Representation Learning for Visual Imitation.* [online at arxiv.org].

Peffers, K., T. Tuunanen, M.A. Rothenberger, and S. Chatterjee. 2008. "A Design Science Research Methodology for Information Systems Research." *Journal of Management Information Systems* 24, no. 3, pp. 45–77. [online at citeseerx .ist.psu.edu].

Pichai, S.. 2018. "AI at Google: Our Principles." *The Keyword* 7, pp. 1–3.

Prahalad, C.K., and R.A. Bettis. 1986. "The Dominant Logic: A New Linkage Between Diversity And Performance." *Strategic Management Journal* 7, no. 6, pp. 485–501. [online at deepblue.lib.umich.edu].

Prahalad, C.K., and R.A. Bettis. 2000. "The Dominant Logic: A New Linkage Between Diversity And Performance." In J.A.C. Baum, and F. Dobbin. ed. *Economics Meets Sociology in Strategic Management (Advances in Strategic Management, Vol. 17)*, pp. 119–141. Emerald Group Publishing Limited, Bingley. [online at deepblue.lib.umich.edu].

Ratcliffe, S. 2017. *Oxford Essential Quotations (5 ed.).* Oxford University Press. [online at oxfordreference.com].

Rainie, L., C. Funk, M. Anderson, and A. Tyson. March 17, 2022. "AI and Human Enhancement: Americans' Openness Is Tempered by a Range of Concerns." *Public Views Are Tied to How These Technologies Would Be Used, What Constraints Would Be in Place.* Pew Research. [online at pewresearch.org].

Reckwitz, A. 2002. "Toward a Theory of Social Practices: A Development in Culturalist Theorizing." *European Journal of Social Theory* 5, no. 2, pp. 243–263.

Reese, B., and S. Hoffman. 2021. *Wasted: How We Squander Time, Money, and Natural Resources—and What We Can Do About It.* Currency.

Reynolds, E. 2018. "The Agony of Sophia, the World's First Robot Citizen Condemned to a Lifeless Career in Marketing: Sophia the Robot Was Given the Gift of Legal Personhood. Her Reward?" *An eternity working in marketing.* [online at wired.co.uk].

Ridley, M. 2011. *The Rational Optimist: How Prosperity Evolves.* Harper Perennial.

Ricketts, J.A. 2007. *Reaching The Goal: How Managers Improve a Services Business Using Goldratt's Theory of Constraints.* IBM Press.

Rodgers, S. 2016. "Jeremiah Owyang on the Collaborative Economy." *Dassault Systemes—Navigate the Future.* [online at blogs.3ds.com].

Ross, J.W., P. Weill, and D. Robertson. 2006. *Enterprise Architecture as Strategy: Creating a Foundation for Business Execution.* Harvard Business Press.

Rouse, W.B., and J.C. Spohrer. 2018. "Automating Versus Augmenting Intelligence." *Journal of Enterprise Transformation* 8, no. 8, pp. 1–21.

Ruskin, J. 1860/1920. *Unto This Last.* E.P. Dutton & Company.

Russell, S. 2019. *Human Compatible: Artificial Intelligence and the Problem of Control.* Viking.

Russell, S. 2021. "Artificial Intelligence and the Problem of Control." In H. Werthner et al. eds., *Perspectives on Digital Humanism*, pp. 19–24. [online at link.springer.com].

Rust, R. 2004. "A Call for a Wider Range of Service Research." *Journal of Service Research* 6, no. 3, pp. 211–211.

Sandkrueler, H.J. 1999. "Enzyklopädie Philosophie O-Z." Article by H.D. Gondek on "Strukturalismus" (Structuralism). Meiner.

Sapjic, D.J. 2019. *The Future of Employment—30 Telling Gig Economy Statistics.* Small Business by the Numbers. [online at smallbizgenius.com].

Saviano, M., F. Polese, F. Caputo, and L. Walletzky. 2016. "A T-shaped Model for Rethinking Higher Education Programs." Proceedings of the 19th Toulon-Verona International Conference "Excellence in Services" at Huelva.

Schon, D.A. 1984. *The Reflective Practitioner: How Professionals Think in Action.* Basic Books.

Schumacher, E.F. 1973/2010. *Small Is Beautiful: Economics as if People Mattered.* Harper Perennial. [summary on wikipedia.org].

Sculley, J., and J.A. Byrne. 1987. *Odyssey: Pepsi to Apple : A Journey of Adventure, Ideas, and the Future.* Harper Collins.

Seabright, P. 2010. *The Company of Strangers: A Natural History of Economic Life.* Revised Edition. Princeton University Press.

Searle, J.R. 1997. *The Construction of Social Reality.* Free Press.

Sen, A. 2000. *Development as Freedom.* Anchor.

Sheffler, K. 2015. *Changing The Lens Of Your Life Through Your Mindset.* [online at www.mindsetmovement.org]

Simon, H.A. 1965. *The Shape of Automation for Men and Management.* Harper & Row.

Simon, H.A. 1996. *The Sciences of the Artificial, Third Edition.* MIT press.

Smith, B., and H. Shum. 2018. *The Future Computed.* Microsoft. [online at Microsoft.com].

Smolin, L. 2014. *Time Reborn: From the Crisis in Physics to the Future of the Universe.* Mariner Books.

Somel, M., X. Liu, and P. Khaitovich. 2013. "Human Brain Evolution: Transcripts, Metabolites and their Regulators." *Nature Reviews Neuroscience* 14, no. 2, pp. 112–127.

Spohrer, J., and P.P. Maglio. May 2008. "The Emergence of Service Science: Toward Systematic Service Innovations to Accelerate Co-Creation of Value." *Production and Operations Management* 17, no. 3, pp. 238–246.

Spohrer, J., S.L. Vargo, N. Caswell, and P.P. Maglio. 2008. "The Service System is the Basic Abstraction of Service Science." Proceedings of the 41st Annual Hawaii International Conference on System Sciences (HICSS 2008). [online at citeseerx.ist.psu.edu].

Spohrer, J.C., and P.P. Maglio. 2010. "Toward a Science of Service System." In *Handbook of Service Science*, Maglio, Kieliszewski, and Spohrer eds., pp. 157–194. Springer.

Spohrer, J., and P.P. Maglio. 2010. "Service Science: Toward a Smarter Planet." In Karwowski, and Salvendy eds., *Introduction to Service Engineering*, pp. 1–33. Wiley & Sons.

Spohrer, J.C., H. Demirkan, and V. Krishna. 2011. "Service and Science." In *The Science of Service Systems*, pp. 325–358. Springer.

Spohrer, J.C. 2011. "On Looking Into Vargo and Lusch's Concept of Generic Actors in Markets, or "It's All B2B... and Beyond!." *Industrial Marketing Management* 2, no. 40, pp. 199–201.

Spohrer, J. 2012. *A New Engineering-Challenge Discipline: Rapidly Rebuilding Societal Infrastructure.* [online at service-science.info].

Spohrer, J., A. Giuiusa, H. Demirkan, and D. Ing. 2013. "Service Science: Reframing Progress With Universities." *Systems Research and Behavioral Science* 30, no. 5, pp. 561–569. [online at coevolving.com].

Spohrer, J., S.K. Kwan, and R.P. Fisk. 2014. "Marketing: A Service Science and Arts Perspective." In Rust and Huang eds., *Handbook of Service Marketing Research*, 489–526.

Spohrer, J., and G. Banavar. December 2015. "Cognition as a Service: An Industry Perspective." *AI Magazine* 36, no. 4, pp. 71–86. [online at aaai.org].

Spohrer, J. 2015. "Empowering Makers in the Cognitive Era." In *Proceedings of the Eleventh Annual International Conference on International Computing Education Research*. [also see online presentation at slideshare.net/spohrer].

Spohrer, J. 2016. "Services Science and Societal Convergence." In W. Bainbridge, M. Roco eds. *Handbook of Science and Technology Convergence*. Springer.

Spohrer, J. January 2017. "IBM's Service Journey: A Summary Sketch." *Industrial Marketing Management* 60, pp. 167–172.

Spohrer, J., M.A. Siddike, Y. Kohda. 2017. "Rebuilding Evolution: A Service Science Perspective." In *Proceedings of the 50th Hawaii International Conference on System Sciences*. [online at https://scholarspace.manoa.hawaii.edu].

Spohrer, J., and M.A.K. Siddike. 2018. "The Future of Digital Cognitive Systems: Tool, Assistant Collaborator, Coach, Mediator." In ed., D. Araya, *Augmented Intelligence: Smart Systems and the Future of Work and Learning*. Peter Lang Publishing.

Spohrer, J. 2019. *An Exciting New Book: Open Innovation Results.* [online at slideshare.net/spohrer].

Spohrer, J. 2020a. *Online Platform Economy and Gig Workers: A USA Perspective.* [online at slideshare.net/spohrer].

Spohrer, J. 2020b. *Augmented Intelligence.* [online at slideshare.net/spohrer].

Spohrer, J. 2020c. *How Will COVID-19 Impact the World of Service Robots?* [online at slideshare.net/spohrer] [also see ISSIP YouTube—June 25, 2020].

Spohrer, J. 2021a. "Service Innovation Roadmaps and Responsible Entities Learning." IESS 2.1. ITM Web of Conferences 38. [online at itm-conferences.org].

Spohrer, J. 2021b. *Transdisciplinary Thinking.* [online at service-science.info].

Spohrer, J. 2021c. *A Service Innovation Whose Time Has Come.* [online at service-science.info].

Spohrer, J. 2022. *Thinking about ServCollab and ISSIP.* [online at service-science.info].

Storbacka, K., R.J. Brodie, T. Böhmann, P.P. Maglio, and S. Nenonen. 2016. "Actor Engagement as a Microfoundation for Value Cocreation." *Journal of Business Research* 69, no. 8, pp. 3008–3017.

Suarez, F.F. 2004. "Battles for Technological Dominance: An Integrative Framework." *Research Policy* 33, no. 2, pp. 271–286. [online at citeseerx.ist.psu.edu].

Tapscott, D., and D. Ticoll. 2012. *The Naked Corporation: How the Age of Transparency Will Revolutionize Business.* Free Press.

Teare, G. 2022. *Global Venture Funding And Unicorn Creation In 2021 Shattered All Records.* [online at crunchable.come].

Teilhard De Chardin, P. 1959. *The Phenomenon of Man.* Harper.

Tennie, C., J. Call, and M. Tomasello. 2009. "Ratcheting Up The Ratchet: On the Evolution of Cumulative Culture." *Philosophical Transactions of the Royal Society B: Biological Sciences* 364, no. 1528, pp. 2405–2415. [online at reseachgate.net].

The Open Group. 2021. *The SOA Source Book.* [online at opengroup.org].

Töhönen, H., M. Heiskala, and T. Männistö. 2011. "Towards the Operationalization of Service Logic." In *Naples Forum on Service.* [online at academic.edu].

Tolman, C.W., F. Cherry, R. van Hezewijk, and I. Lubek. 1996. *Problems of Theoretical Psychology.* Captus.

Torpey, E., and A. Hogan. 2016. *Working in a Gig Economy.* USA Bureau of Labor Statistics. [online at bls.gov].

Turck, M. 2016. *The Power of Data Network Effects.* [online at mattturck.com].

United Nations. 2015. *Transforming Our World: The 2030 Agenda for Sustainable Development.* A/RES/70/1. [online at sdgs.un.org].

van den Bos, W., E. van Dijk, M. Westenberg, S.A.R.B. Rombouts, and E.A. Crone. 2011. "Changing Brains, Changing Perspectives: The Neurocognitive Development of Reciprocity." *Psychological Science* 22, no. 1, pp. 60–70. [online at researchgate.net].

Van Dijck, J., T. Poell, and M. De Waal. 2018. *The Platform Society: Public Values in a Connective World.* Oxford University Press. [book review].

Vargo, S.L., and R.F. Lusch. 2004. "Evolving to a New Dominant Logic for Marketing." *Journal of Marketing* 68, pp. 1–17. [online at www.researchgate.net].

Vargo, S.L., and R.F. Lusch. 2008. "Why Service?" *Journal of the Academy of Marketing Science (JAMS)* 36, pp. 25–38. [online at www.researchgate.net].

Vargo, S.L., and R.F. Lusch. 2016. "Institutions and Axioms: An Extension and Update of Service-Dominant Logic." *Journal of the Academy of Marketing Science* 44, no. 1, pp. 5–23. [online at www.researchgate.net].

Vargo, S.L., and R.F. Lusch. 2017. "Service-Dominant Logic 2025." *International Journal of Research in Marketing* 34, pp. 46–67. [online at sdlogic.net].

Vargo, S.L., and R.F. Lusch. 2018. "The SAGE Handbook of Service-Dominant Logic." SAGE Publications.

Vargo, S.L., and F.W. Morgan. 2019. "Services in Society and Academic Thought: An Historical Analysis," In S.L. Vargo, and R.F. Lusch eds., *Sage Handbook on Service-Dominant Logic, (reprinted from Journal of Micromarketing)*, pp. 22–39.

Vargo, S.L., L. Peters, H. Kjellberg, K. Koskela-Houtari, S. Nenonen, F. Polese, D. Sarno, and C. Vaughan. 2022. "Emergence in Marketing: An Institutional and Ecosystem Framework." *Journal of the Academy Marketing Science*. [online at springer.com].

Vink, J., B. Tronvoll, B. Edvardsson, K. Wetter-Edman, and M. Aguirre. 2017. "Service Ecosystem Design: Doing Institutional Work Through Design." Naples Forum on Service Conference. [online at naplesforumonservice.com].

Wadhwa, V. 2016. "The Amazing Artificial Intelligence We Were Promised is Coming, Finally." Washington Post online, Opinion, Innovation. [online at washingtonpost.com].

Ward, M. December 04, 2020. "Billionaire Investor Bill Ackman Says the US Should Give Every American Cash at Birth So They Can Retire a Millionaire." Insider. [online at www.businessinsider.com].

Warg, M., P. Weiss, and R. Engel. 2015, in German. *Service Dominierte Architektur (SDA): Die Digitale Transformation Erfolgreich Meistern.* [online at researchgate.net].

Warg, M., and R. Engel. 2016. "Service-Dominierte Architektur (SDA): Kernkomponente Digitaler Transformation." *Zeitschrift für Versicherungswesen*, no. 12, pp. 391–395. [online at researchgate.net].

Warg, M., and R. Engel. 2016. *Service Dominant Architecture (SDA): A Building Block of Digital Transformation.* [online at researchgate.net].

Warg, M., P. Weiss, R. Engel, and A. Zolnowski. 2016. "Service Dominant Architecture Based on S-D Logic for Mastering Digital Transformation: The Case of an Insurance Company." Paper presented at the 26th Annual RESER Conference, Naples, Italy. [online at researchgate.net].

Warg, M., M.W. Frosch, P. Weiss, and A. Zolnowski. 2018. "Becoming a Platform Organization—How Incumbent Companies Stay Competitive." *Cutter Business Technology Journal* 31, no. 11.

Warg, M., A. Zolnowski, M. Frosch, and P. Weiss. 2019. *From Product Organization to Platform Organization—Observations of Organizational Development in the Insurance Industry.* Naples Forum on Service.

Warg, M. July 16–20, 2020. "Architecture and Its Multifaceted Roles in Enabling Value Cocreation in the Context of Human-Centered Service Design." In eds. J. Spohrer, and C. Leitner, *Advances in the Human Side of Service Engineering: Proceedings of the AHFE 2020 Virtual Conference on The Human Side of Service Engineering.* [online at researchgate.net].

Warg, M., and S. Hans. 2021. "How to Overcome Organizational Inertia by Shaping Institutions and Value Propositions: An Analysis of the Impact of Service-Catalogs." 31st RESER Conference, I.A.O. Fraunhofer, and Heilbronn, 2021 in: *The Disruptive Role of Data, AI and Ecosystems in Services, Conference Proceedings of 31th RESER Conference*, B. Bienzeisler, K. Peters, and A. Schletz. [online at www.ifsd.hamburg].

Warg, M. 2021. *Service in the AI Era.* [online at www.ifsd.hamburg].

WEF. 2017. *Towards a Reskilling Revolution—A Future of Jobs For All.* World Economic Forum. [online at www.weforum.org].

Weick, K.E. 1995. "Sensemaking in Organization (Foundations for Organizational Science)." Sage.

Weiss, P., A. Zolnowski, M. Warg, and T. Schuster. 2018. "Service Dominant Architecture: Conceptualizing the Foundation for Execution of Digital Strategies Based on SD Logic." In Proceedings of the 51st Hawaii International Conference on System Sciences. [online at hawaii.edu].

Weiss, P., M. Warg, and A. Zolnowski. 2019. "Building Systems of Engagement to Overcome the Challenges of Digital Transformation." In Proceedings of 10th Naples Forum on Service, June Istia IT. ISSIP Best Paper Award. [online at researchgate.net].

Wenger-Trayner, E., and B. Wenger-Trayner. 2015. *Communities of Practice: A Brief Introduction.* [online at wenger-trayner.com].

West, S., P. Gaiardelli, B. Resta, and D. Kujawski. January 01, 2018. "Co-Creation of Value in Product-Service Systems Through Transforming Data Into Knowledge." *IFAC-PapersOnLine* 51, no. 11, pp. 1323–1328. [online at researchgate.net].

West, S., J. Meierhofer, O. Stoll, and L. Schweiger. 2020. "Value Propositions Enabled by Digital Twins in the Context of Servitization." *Advanced Services for Sustainability and Growth. Proceedings of Spring Sustainability Conference*, pp. 152–160. [online at flore.unifi.it].

West, S., O. Stoll, J. Meierhofer, and S. Züst. 2021. "Digital Twin Providing New Opportunities for Value Co-Creation Through Supporting Decision-Making." *Applied Sciences* 11, no. 9, pp. 3750–3783.[online at mdpi-res.com].

West, S., W. Zou, E. Rodel, and O. Stoll. 2021. "Value Co-Creation in Digitally-Enabled Product-Service Systems." In *The Palgrave Handbook of Servitization*, pp. 403–417. Palgrave Macmillan.

West, S., Y. Keiser, O. Stoll, and S. Züst. 2022. "Exploring Factory Digital Production Support System Through the Lens of Service-Dominant Logic." In *ITM Web of Conferences 2022.EDP Sciences* 41, p. 04002. [online at itm-conferences.org].

Whitehead, A.N. 1911/2012. "An Introduction to Mathematics." *Project Gutenberg Ebook 2012*. London: Original 1911 book published by Williams & Norgate. [online at gutenberg.org].

Whiten, A. and D. Erdal. 2012. "The Human Socio-Cognitive Niche and Its Evolutionary Origins." *Philosophical Transactions of the Royal Society B: Biological Sciences* 367, no. 1599, pp. 2119–2129. [online at researchgate.net].

Wirtz, J. 2020. "Be Prepared for the Service Revolution." Feature Story: Singapore Institute of Directors Bulletin. [online at researchgate.net].

Wirtz, J., W.H. Kunz, and S. Paluch. 2021. *The Service Revolution, Intelligent Automation and Service Robots*. [online at researchgate.net].

Wirtz, J., and C. Lovelock. 2021. *Services Marketing: People, Technology, Strategy*. World Scientific Publishing Company.

Wladalsky-Berger, I. 2022. *The Widening Gap Between Technological and Institutional Change*. [online at blog.irvingwb.com].

Wright, R. 2001. *Nonzero: The Logic of Human Destiny*. Vintage.

Zizu. 2018. "Dartmouth Workshop: The Birthplace Of AI." Published in RLA Academy. [online at medium.com/rla-academy].

Zolnowski, A., and M. Warg. 2018. "Conceptualizing Resource Orchestration—The Role of Service Platforms in Facilitating Service Systems." Paper presented at the 51st Hawaii International Conference on System Sciences (HICSS-51). [online at scholarspace.manoa.hawaii.edu].

Zysman, J. July 2006. "The Algorithmic Revolution? The Fourth Service Transformation." *Communications of the ACM. Special issue on Services Science* 49, no. 7, p. 49.

About the Authors

Jim Spohrer is a retired IBM executive and active in the International Society of Service Innovation Professionals (ISSIP.org). He has a bachelor's degree in physics from MIT and a PhD in Computer Science/Artificial Intelligence from Yale. One of the founders of the field of service science, with over 90 publications and nine patents, his awards include AMA ServSIG Christopher Lovelock Career Contributions to the Service Discipline, Evert Gummesson Service Research, Vargo-Lusch Service-Dominant Logic, Daniel Berg Service Systems, and PICMET Fellow for advancing service science.

Paul P. Maglio is a Professor of Management and Cognitive Science at the University of California, Merced. He has a bachelor's degree in computer science and engineering from MIT and a PhD in cognitive science from the University of California, San Diego. One of the founders of the field of service science, Dr. Maglio was the Editor-in-Chief of *INFORMS Service Science* (2013–2018), and is Lead Editor of the *Handbook of Service Science, Volumes I and II*. He has published more than 125 papers in computer science, cognitive science, and service science.

Stephen L. Vargo is a Shidler Distinguished Professor and Professor of Marketing at the University of Hawai'i at Manoa. He has published in the *Journal of Marketing, Journal of the Academy of Marketing Science, Journal of Consumer Research, Journal of Service Research, MIS Quarterly*, and other top-ranked journals, in addition to three books. He currently serves as the Editor-in-Chief of the *AMS Review* and is on the editorial/advisory boards of 17 other journals. Professor Vargo has been awarded the Shelby D. Hunt/Harold H. Maynard Award (twice) and the AMA/Sheth Foundation Award for his contributions to marketing theory, as well as the Christopher Lovelock Career Contributions Award, among other recognitions. The Web of Science Group has named him to its *Highly Cited Researchers* list (top 1%) in impact in economics and business, worldwide, for each of the last eight years.

Markus Warg is a Professor for Leadership, Service Design, and Risk Management at University of Applied Sciences Wedel/Hamburg. He has a degree in economics and doctorates in business administration. In 2015, Warg published the Service Dominant Architecture (SDA), is the Chairman of the supervisory board of SDA SE and heading the Institut für Service Design, Hamburg.

Index

Agent, 55, 73, 85
Alexander, Christopher, 35, 89
All models are wrong, 75
Animal rights, 80
Application, 41, 56, 87, *See also*
    diligence
    of knowledge, 13, 18–19, 39, 62,
      76
    of resources, 45, 48, 55, 67
Appropriate technology, 82
Architecture, 88–91
    dominant, 37–38, 91–92
    foundations, 37–38, 91–92
    questions, 43, 98–99
    service dominant architecture
      (SDA), 39–42, 93–98
Arndt, Johann, 25, 84
Artificial general intelligence (AGI),
    63
Artificial intelligence (AI)
    digital service twin, 45–46, 99–102
    foundations, 3–4, 69–70
    future perspectives, 63–64
    investment, 50–54
    platform society, 71–72
    questions, 9–10, 72–74
    reality *vs.* vision, 46–50
    service robots, 70–71
Augmentation. *See* augmented
    cognition and intelligence
    amplification
Augmented cognition, 3–4, 69–70
Autocatalytic set, 61
Automation, 3–6, 8, 9, 10, 52,
    68–70, 73, 86, 93

Becoming, xviii, xix, 16, 18, 22, 27,
    33, 37, 46, 53, 56, 58, 63,
    65, 102
Benefits, 16, 41–43, 45, 48, 51, 55,
    62, 63, 67, 79, 87, 98

of digital twins, 101
of human-level AI, 101
mutual, 18, 30, 61, 76
organizational, 40
of S-D logic, 31
Bicentennial Man (film), 19, 79
Box, George E.P., 11
Brain, 46, 48, 68
Business, xix, xx, xxii, 3, 5, 7–9,
    13–16, 18, 19, 21, 22, 33,
    38–43, 46, 50–53, 60, 64, 65,
    66, 68, 69, 70–75, 77, 78, 80,
    82–86, 92, 93, 97, 99, 103

Capital platforms, 8
Change. *See* Impermanence,
    Becoming, and Process
    Philosophy
Civilization, xiii, 68, 83, 90
Cocreation, xx, xxi, 16, 17, 30–31,
    33, 41, 42, 52, 55, 57, 60, 87,
    90, 93–96
Coercion, 16, 37
Cognitive map, 86
Common knowledge, 85
Commons, 88
Community, xvii, xviii, xix, xxx, 34,
    15, 59, 64, 65, 67, 69, 80, 82,
    84–87
Community of practice, xvi, 3, 4, 15,
    28, 45, 55, 73, 76, 77, 84–86,
    99
Company, xviii, 10, 39, 40, 41, 53,
    80, 82, 92, 97, 100, *See also*
    Multinational corporation
    and start-up company
Competition, 18, 43, 49
Complexity economics, 22, 43, 78
Compliance. *See* Regulatory
    compliance

Component Business Model (CBM), 92
Computational models, 64
Conflict resolution, 101
Contract, 46
Cooperation, xii, 28, 43, 61, 78
Corporate personhood, 80
Culture, xviii, 15, 17, 18, 49, 57, 59, 78, 82, 84, 85
Curiosity, xvii, 5, 58, 64, 81, 82, 102
Customer, xix, xx, xxi, 5–8, 21, 22, 40, 41, 49, 50–52, 67, 68, 70, 71, 84, 87, 94, 96, 97
Customer engagement, 7
Customer value proposition, 41, 96

Data architecture, 96–97
Data (Star Trek), 69, 79
Dartmouth workshop, 69
Decision-making, 22, 85
Design, xxi, xxii, 22, 31, 35–41, 76, 80, 88–91, 95, 97, 100
Design pattern, 37–41, 91, 94, 95
Development, 13, 39, 74, 81, 85, 86, 98
Digital attacker platform architecture, 40, 93
Digital service, xix, 7, 66
Digital service twin, 45–46, 99–102
Digital transformation, 39, 41, 42, 93, 97
Digital twin, 22, 45, 46, 55, 56, 60, 63, 64, 71, 73, 74, 99, 100, 101
Dispute resolution, 16
Dominance, 29, 92
Dominant architectures, 38
Dominant design, 38, 43, 91–92
Dominant logic, 27–28, 84–85

Ecology, 13, 15–17, 19, 53, 56, 61, 77–79, 99
Ecosystem, 30–31, 33, 41, 42, 87, 90, 92, 97, 99, See also Digital ecosystem
Educator. See Professor and Teacher
Einstein, Albert, 25, 84
Emergence, 61, 62, 70, 90

of digital attacker platform architecture, 40, 93
of multinational enterprise architecture, 92
of service dominant architecture (SDA), 41–42, 93
of service-oriented architecture (SOA), 39-40, 93
of value propositions, 94
Enterprise. See Company, State-Owned Enterprise
Enterprise architecture, 35, 37–41, 45, 55, 88, 91–93, 99, 103
Entity, 1, 69, 97, See also Named entity
Entrepreneurship, 18, 49, 65, 68
Ethics, xx, xxi
Everyday life, xvii, xix, 62

Family, xviii, 6, 16, 48
Fear, xix, xxi, xxii, 8, 75, 102
Foster, Norman, 35, 88
Freedom, xxii

Game theory, 61
Giddens, Anthony, 36, 90
Goods-dominant (G-D) logic, 29, 45, 55
Group, 85

Habit, xvii, 53, 102
Health equity, 23, 49, 52, 56, 63, 101, 102
Household, 70

Identity, xii
Imitation, 3, 48, 101
Impermanence, 65–67
Income earner, 8, 22
Individual, xxii, 29, 50, 51, 53, 72, 75, 80, 99, 102
Information, xii
Information and Communication Technologies (ICT), 92
Information Technology (IT), 92, 99
Innovation, 4, 5, 14, 16, 52, 53, 55, 66–67, 70, 71, 98, 102

Institutions, xii, 22, 30, 35, 41, 45, 48, 65, 71, 81, 88–90, 94, 95, 97, 99
Institutional economics, 93
Interaction, xvii–xxii, 7, 15–19, 27, 33, 41, 45, 46, 49, 50, 53, 55–57, 60–62, 65–67, 72, 76, 78, 79, 84, 85, 87, 94–96, 98, 102

Jakobson, Roman, 36, 90
Justice, xxii

Key Performance Indicators (KPI), 92
Knowledge, xii, 10, 13, 14, 16–18, 23, 29, 39, 45, 48, 52, 55–57, 61–64, 73, 76–78, 80, 82, 83, 85, 87, 90, 93, 94
Knowledge-driven value cocreation, 30–31, 33, 87
Knowledge representation and reasoning, 85
Kries, Mateo, 36, 89

Labor platforms, 8
Law, 1, 68, 70, 72, 75, 76
L(earners). See learning and income earner
Learning, xii, xvii, xix, xxi, 3, 10, 18, 19, 22, 37, 47–50, 52, 53, 56, 64, 67, 73, 74, 80, 85, 88, 90, 97, 100–102
Legal entity, 15
Lego construction, 97
Lewin, Kurt, 35, 88
Logic, 41–43, 45, 46, 50. 55–57, 60, 64, 92, 93, 94, 98, 102, 103, See also Common knowledge; Mental model; Paradigm
dominant, 27–28, 84–85
foundations, 27–28, 84–85
questions, 33, 87–88
service-dominant logic, 29–31, 86–87

Machine, xx, 1, 3, 8, 9, 39, 63, 67, 82
Mediation, xix, 46
Mental model, 27, 29, 30, 85, 86

Mind, xvii, xxii, 46, 48, 70, 85
Mindset, 27, 30, 31, 38, 65, 86, 87
Model, xii, 7, 8, 13, 15, 16, 18, 21, 22, 23, 27, 29, 30, 40, 42, 45, 46, 48–54, 56, 59, 63, 64, 73, 74, 77, 78, 84–86, 92, 93, 97, 101, 102
Monster truck, xix
Multinational corporation, 92
Mutual benefits, 18, 30, 48, 61, 76
Mutual value creation, 31, 93, 94, 97

Naïve physics, 85
Named entity, 15
Newtonian mechanics, 27

Observational learning, 101
Occupational Information Network (O*NET), 100
Online platform, 66
Organization, xii, , xx, 22, 29, 37, 38, 41, 42, 50, 57, 69, 85, 88, 91–93, 98, 99, 102, See also legal entity, company, institution, and voluntary association
Ostrom, Elinor, 88–89
Outcome, xvii, 7, 15–17, 19, 29, 30, 45, 51, 53, 55, 56, 57, 59, 60, 72, 84, 87, 90, 100

Papanek, Victor, 35, 88
Paradigm, 11, 25, 27, 39, 76, 86, 87
Paradigm shift, 28
Pattern language, 89, See also design patterns
People, xi, xvii–xxii, 4, 5, 7, 9, 13–16, 18, 19, 21, 23, 39, 45–52, 57, 62, 63, 64, 66, 68, 70, 71, 75, 76, 78, 81, 84–88, 99, 100, 102
Platform economy, xxi, 7–8, 42, 70–72, 71, 95, 97
Platform organization. See platform economy
Platform society. See platform economy
Point-of-view, 55, 85, 94

Practitioner, xx, xxi, 5, 9, 13, 21, 22,
    31, 33, 38, 43, 47, 50–52, 64,
    72, 80, 85, 87, 101, 102, *See
    also* Worker; Professional
Process philosophy, 90
Productivity, xx, xxi, 3, 14, 16, 55,
    69, 71, 72, 77, 92
Professional, xx, 3, 4, 17, 60, 64, 72,
    76, 79
Professor, 73, 76
Progress in AI, xxii, 46, 63, 68
Promise, 16, 55, 56, 78, 98

Quality, xx, 4, 13, 14, 16, 52, 55, 68,
    77, 81
Quality-of-life (QOL), xvii, 37, 66,
    72
Quantum mechanics, 27

Recommender system, 7
Reflective practice, 64
Regulatory compliance, xx, 14, 16, 41
Resource, 30, 31, 35, 53
Resource density, 40–42, 94, 95
Responsibility, xx, xxi, xxii, 75
Reputation, xii
Researcher, 46, 64, 85
Resources, xii
Ross, Jeanne W., 35, 88, 92

Schema, 86
Scholar, xx, xxi, 10, 23, 31, 33, 38,
    43, 47, 48, 50, 51, 52, 53, 64,
    79, 82, 84, 85, 87, 101, 102,
    See also Researcher
Schumacher, E.F., 82
Science, xix, xxii, 3, 11–23, 27, 43,
    45, 46, 50, 64, 69, 75–83, 85,
    86, 88
  foundations, 13–14, 77
  questions, 21–23, 80–83
  service science, 15–19, 77–80
Self-service technologies (SSTs), 4,
    70, 74
Sensemaking, 85
Service, xi–xiii, 55–56
  centrality, xi, 60–61
  phenomenon, xiii, 62

Service catalog, 97
Service design, 97
Service dominant architecture (SDA),
    39–43, 45, 56, 57, 60, 93–98,
    103, *See also* Dominant design
Service-dominant (S-D) logic, 29–30,
    56, 57, 86–87
Service ecosystems, 30–31, 87, 98
Service-for-service exchange, 55–56
Service innovation, xiv, 5, 13, 41, 53,
    57, 66, 67, 70, 74, 98, xix
Service-oriented architecture (SOA),
    39–40, 88, 92, 93
Service platforms, 98
Service provision, 29
Service robot, xx, 4–8, 70–72, 74
Service Science, Management, and
    Engineering, 15–19, 21–23,
    31, 39, 41, 42, 45, 56, 57, 60,
    65, 70, 76–82, 93, 98, 103
Six Degrees of Kevin Bacon, xi–xiii
Social design, 36, 89, 90, *See also*
    social entrepreneurship
Social equity, 23, 49, 52, 56, 63, 101,
    102
Social exclusion, 23, 49, 52, 56, 63,
    101, 102
Social learning. *See* Imitation,
    Observational learning, and
    Social learning theory
Social learning theory, 101
Social robot, 70
Society, xx, xxi, 3, 7–8, 23, 29, 37,
    50, 57, 58, 62, 70–72, 77, 82,
    89, 97, 102, 103
Socio-technical system, 76, 79, 80
Sophia (robot), 79
Startup company, 10, 43
Structuration theory, 90
Sustainable Development Goals, 51,
    101
System, 13, 16, 22, 29, 30, 42, 46,
    49, 61, 67, 82, 83, 90, 94–96

Teacher, 3, 101
Technological determinism, 50
Technology, xii, xiii, xix, 3–5, 7, 42,
    45, 46, 48, 53, 59, 66, 77, 81,
    82, 98, 102

Telerobotics, 6, 8

The Open Group, 92

The Open Group Architectural
Framework (TOGAF), 92

Theory of the mind, 48

Time, 7, 8, 37, 43, 53, 66, 84, 88,
102

Transdisciplinarity, 17–19, 23, 52, 53,
73, 79–80, 102

Trust, xii, xx, 14, 18, 23, 46, 81, 82

T-shaped skills, 17, 79, 100

Under-served populations, *See* health
equity, social equity, and
social exclusion

Understanding, xvii, xviii, xix, xxii,
18, 23, 27, 28, 30, 36, 48, 50,
53, 60, 69, 75, 78, 79, 82, 88,
90, 95, 97, 98, 101–103

Utility, 21, 23, 29, 52

Value, xi, xxii, 13, 29, 30, 42, 51, 57,
66, 73, 83, 86–87, 94

Value proposition, 16, 17, 23, 41, 56,
78, 94, 96–98

Vendor, 40, 87

Well-being, xvii, xviii, xxii, 29, 30, 37,
65, 72, 75, 83, 102

Winner takes all, xxi, 67

Winner take all market, xxi, 67

Winner take most. *See* Winner take all
market

Worker, 9

OTHER TITLES IN THE SERVICE SYSTEMS AND INNOVATIONS IN BUSINESS AND SOCIETY COLLECTION

Jim Spohrer, IBM, and Haluk Demirkan, University of Washington, Tacoma, Editors

- *The Emergent Approach to Strategy* by Peter Compo
- *Compassion-Driven Innovation* by Nicole Reineke, Debra Slapak, and Hanna Yehuda
- *Adoption and Adaption in Digital Business* by Keith Sherringham and Bhuvan Unhelkar
- *Customer Value Starvation Can Kill* by Walter Vieira
- *Build Better Brains* by Martina Muttke
- *ATOM, Second Edition* by Kartik Gada
- *Designing Service Processes to Unlock Value, Third Edition* by Joy M. Field
- *Disruptive Innovation and Digital Transformation* by Marguerite L. Johnson
- *Service Excellence in Organizations, Volume II* by Fiona Urquhart
- *Service Excellence in Organizations, Volume I* by Fiona Urquhart
- *Obtaining Value from Big Data for Service Systems, Volume II* by Stephen H. Kaisler, Armour, and J. Alberto Espinosa
- *Obtaining Value from Big Data for Service Systems, Volume I* by Stephen H. Kaisler, Armour, and J. Alberto Espinosa

Concise and Applied Business Books

The Collection listed above is one of 30 business subject collections that Business Expert Press has grown to make BEP a premiere publisher of print and digital books. Our concise and applied books are for...

- Professionals and Practitioners
- Faculty who adopt our books for courses
- Librarians who know that BEP's Digital Libraries are a unique way to offer students ebooks to download, not restricted with any digital rights management
- Executive Training Course Leaders
- Business Seminar Organizers

Business Expert Press books are for anyone who needs to dig deeper on business ideas, goals, and solutions to everyday problems. Whether one print book, one ebook, or buying a digital library of 110 ebooks, we remain the affordable and smart way to be business smart. For more information, please visit www.businessexpertpress.com, or contact sales@businessexpertpress.com.

www.ingramcontent.com/pod-product-compliance
Lightning Source LLC
Chambersburg PA
CBHW061324220326
41599CB00026B/5015